LITERATURE AND
THE RISE OF CAPITALISM

LITERATURE AND THE RISE OF CAPITALISM

Critical Essays
mainly on the Sixteenth and Seventeenth Centuries

by

RAYMOND SOUTHALL

1973
LAWRENCE & WISHART
LONDON

SBN 0 85315 268 3

Printed in Great Britain by
The Camelot Press Ltd, London and Southampton

TO RICHARD

Wer andere bekrittelt arbeitet an seiner Selbstbesserung

SCHOPENHAUER

Contents

Preface

Although the following essays were produced at different times and in different circumstances, they share a common concern for the ways in which the rise of capitalism made itself felt in our literature. Between the prologue (on More) and the epilogue (on Johnson) the essays grouped themselves naturally around the initial enthusiasm, the subsequent questioning and the final despair and resolution with which the literature of the sixteenth and seventeenth centuries responded to social change.

Whatever shortcomings are discovered in the following pages would have been far more numerous but for the help I have received from discussion with friends and colleagues. Above all, however, I owe that enormous debt of knowledge and understanding which every teacher owes to his students and I thank them for it even while I realise that I have lost their freshness of vision and can only hint at their wider concern for the social implications of the subject I teach.

Some of the material which appears in the following pages has already appeared in *Essays in Criticism, Marxism Today* and *Shakespeare in A Changing World* (ed. Arnold Kettle, Lawrence and Wishart, 1964). I wish to express my gratitude to the publishers for their permission to reproduce that material here.

R. S.

I

More's *Utopia*: the case for a Palace Revolution

A survey of twentieth-century views of Thomas More leaves a remarkably parti-coloured impression of his character.* To some he is the strict disciplinarian who spent four years in a monastery and who, throughout his life, wore a hair shirt next to his skin; the man responsible for burning several heretics and for publishing virulent attacks upon the Protestant Reformers, Luther and Tyndale. To others he is the cautious conservative, the More *persona* of *Utopia*, who sought to alleviate contemporary evils by means of personal influence and due process; the man who replaced Wolsey in the hope of preventing, or at least minimising, the break with Rome and its consequences. To many he is primarily the humanist, liberal-minded, progressive and humane, disciple of his old confessor Colet and lifelong friend of Erasmus. To these last he appears as the enlightened *paterfamilias* and as the man who tried to dissuade rioting London apprentices from assaulting foreign artisans and their families on Evil May Day and who intervened in the King's name to protect the Oxford humanists from the attacks of their conservative colleagues. On this view he appears ultimately a tragic figure, whose good intentions led him to eventual martyrdom. For some he is the spokesman of the London merchants, the M.P. who opposed the financial exactions of Henry VIII in the House of Commons; the man who represented the guild of Mercers in the Low Countries so well that he was made a member of the guild, an under-sheriff of London, and was returned to the Low Countries to represent the interests of the English wool trade, later being appointed to negotiate with the merchants of the Hanseatic League. To these he is the honest and respected bourgeois. To yet others he is a revolutionary social critic and prophet of the classless society,† a man who eventually

* *Twentieth Century Interpretations of Utopia*, ed. William Nelson (Prentice-Hall, Englewood Cliffs, N.J., 1968) provides a good survey. It includes an extract from Karl Kautsky's *Thomas More and His Utopia*.

† There is a better case for arguing that in *Utopia*, Book II, More is the prophet of the kibbutz.

died because he could not compromise with the forces he felt to be responsible for the misery and impoverishment of the commoners of England. The impression gained of More's character from such a brief survey of twentieth-century views is that he was, as one of his contemporaries remarked, "a man for all seasons", a verdict which has received the imprimatur of the film industry.

There is little doubt that More was indeed a man of variety, although many critics have failed to give this due weight, and it is quite conceivable that he could have replied to the diversity of critical opinion of his character in the words of another of his contemporaries, Thomas Wyatt:

> Eche man me telleth I chaunge moost my devise,
>   And on my faith me think it goode reason
>   To chaunge propose like after the season,
>   Ffor in every cas to kepe still oon gyse
> Ys mytt for theim that would be taken wyse;
>   And I ame not of such maner condition,
>   But treted after a dyvers fasshion;
>   And therupon my dyversnes doeth rise.[1]

The strong impression of More's 'dyversnes' carried away from a survey of his critics is largely due to the fact that he too has been "treted after a dyvers fasshion". Critics have approached More from different points of interest, sometimes being unnecessarily contentious in the process. Many, for instance, have urged that More's basic concern in *Utopia* is economic—and certainly the condition of England at the time was such that only the most obtuse social commentator could have ignored the effect of economic change upon the established patterns of English social life. One or two critics, however, have contested this view and have argued that More's basic concern in *Utopia* is a moral one. J. H. Hexter, in his book *More's Utopia: The Biography of an Idea*, believes that More sees the economic evils of his society as a consequence of the sin of pride, and I doubt if any sensible reader would contest this: More does appear to believe that men desire riches in order to gratify an impulse to be thought better than their neighbours and that men bestow respect upon riches because pride is a general human sin. This tendency to move from the concrete social evil to a moral abstraction is by no means uncommon; Pope, for instance, also attacks the sin of pride as the root of most of the social evils of his day. But this *is* an abstraction and to some extent it is an abstraction from the understanding which More makes available to us in *Utopia*. Although we may agree that men pursue riches in order to gratify a desire to be thought better than their neighbours, as More apparently believed,[2] it nevertheless still remains to be explained why men think that riches make them better than their neighbours and why their neighbours accept this evaluation of worth. Quite evidently men believe this because wealth enables them to enlarge their possessions— they can dress in silk and jewels, like the ambassadors to *Utopia*,[3] purchase estates, enjoy fine food, employ servants. Surely the moralist will agree with this explanation of the mystique of wealth? But if it is agreed, then further agreement is entailed; for it follows that wealth is honoured only when it can be converted into money—that is, when it can be used for the purchase of goods. In short, wealth is honorific to the extent that it represents purchasing power. Consequently, wealth becomes a source of pride only in a money economy. More recognises this; he is concerned not with Society but with *a* society, in which, as he puts it, "money beareth all the stroke", a society of rising rents and rising prices, where "rich men . . . buy all to engross and forestall, and with their monopoly to keep the market alone as please them".[4]

In such a society it is, as he sees, money that gives both form and substance to vanity and vice: "where money beareth all the swing there many vain and superfluous occupations must needs be used, to serve only for riotous superfluity and unhonest pleasure".[5] The utopian solution is to abolish private property and thereby to destroy the money economy, even to "procure to have gold and silver . . . in reproach and infamy", for "when all the desire of money with the use thereof is utterly secluded and banished, how great a heap of cares is cut away. . . . Yea, poverty itself, which only seemed to lack money, if money were gone it also would decrease and vanish away. . . . So easily might men get their living, if that same worthy princess Lady Money did not alone stop up the way between us and our living."[6]

Excepting one or two acid remarks upon usury, More's critique of a money economy is an attack upon mercantilism, just as Marx's critique of the formation of capital is an attack upon capitalism. So that whilst it is true that More is preoccupied with the sin of pride, it is not pride in physical prowess, personal beauty, or intellectual ability which concerns him, but that pride which is unleashed by mercantilism and the growth of a money economy. It is this pride and not a moral or theological abstraction which he sees in *Utopia* as the source of the social evils of his time.

It is this social understanding, brought to bear upon the discussion of justice and the law, which (not surprisingly since More was himself a lawyer) occupies so much attention in *Utopia*, the first book setting forth the injustices of contemporary English laws and the second book providing a model of a more equitable state. For More, as later for Marx, the laws of contemporary society are expressions of the dictatorship which one class exercises over the whole people and the means by which it safeguards the fruits and ensures the rights of exploitation. This is one of the firmest conclusions of *Utopia* and the one most forcibly and levelly expressed:

> when I consider and weigh in my mind all the commonwealths which nowadays anywhere do flourish, so God help me, I can perceive nothing but a certain conspiracy of rich men procuring their own commodities under the name and title of the commonwealth. They invent and devise all means and crafts, first how to keep safely, without fear of losing, that they have unjustly gathered together, and next how to hire and abuse the work and labour of the poor for as little as may be. These devices, when the rich men have decreed to be kept and observed under colour of the commonalty,* that is to say, also of the poor people, then they be made laws.[7]

There are those who have argued that More is being ironic throughout the second book of *Utopia*, but the tone of such a passage as this and the full implications of the oath, "so God help me", does not support that argument. There is much humour and some irony in the book, but it seems highly unlikely that More is using that phrase ironically. It seems equally evident that we are not expected to take the sympathy expressed in the paragraph which immediately follows that last as an insincerity. Indeed, the indignation which it expresses is of the very essence of More's humanity:

> And that you may perceive this more plainly, consider with yourselves some barren and unfruitful year wherein many thousands of people have starved for hunger. I dare be bold to say that in the end of that penury so much corn or grain might have been found in the rich men's barns, if they had been searched, as, being divided among them whom famine and pestilence then consumed, no man at all should have felt that plague and penury.[8]

* *The commonalty*: in the national interest, as the same humbugs say today.

The spirit of that passage is the same spirit that we meet with in the uncontestedly serious description of the plight of those impoverished by the enclosures:

> either by hook or crook, they must needs depart away, poor silly, wretched souls, men, women, husbands, wives, fatherless children, widows, woeful mothers with their young babes, and their whole household small in substance and much in number, as husbandry requireth many hands. Away they trudge, I say, out of their own and accustomed houses, finding no place to rest in. All their household stuff, which is very little worth though it might well abide the sale, yet being suddenly thrust out they be constrained to sell it for a thing of nought. And when they have wandered abroad till that be spent, what can they then else do but steal, and then justly pardy be hanged, or else go about a-begging? And yet then also they be cast in prison as vagabonds, because they go about and work not, whom no man will set a-work, though they never so willingly profer themselves thereto.[9]

There is one ironic comment in this description when, having shown how the homeless are reduced to poverty, More asks, "What can they else do but steal, and then justly pardy be hanged?" He is quite obviously being ironic here: the thieves are certainly hanged in accordance with the law, but their punishment is not a just one, as he argues at length in Book I. Such an irony, however, does not call into doubt the sincerity of More's indignation but gives it a finer, sharper edge.

It may be, of course, that More intended *Utopia* as a joke,* an ironic send-up, or that he intended it as a sermon on pride, but he achieved something quite different. It is impossible to treat the work as a consistent irony without calling into doubt More's humanity, and there is nothing within the work to suggest that we should do this, despite the historical limitations of that humanity. It is likewise impossible to view the work in morally or theologically abstract terms, for the evils with which it concerns itself are too socially specific. Furthermore, the whole gist of the argument in Book I and the whole point of Book II is that human nature can be changed by changing human conditions. In Book I it is argued very forcibly that society, by its economic and legal

---

* Erasmus, who knew More's love of a straight-faced joke, didn't think so, however. In his letter to Hutten he declared that More "published his *Utopia* for the purpose of showing, what are the things that occasion mischief in commonwealths; having the English Constitution especially in view".

arrangements (that conspiracy of the rich), creates the criminals it executes:

> Doubtless unless you find a remedy for these enormities you shall in vain advance yourselves of executing justice upon fellons . . . what other thing do you than make thieves and then punish them?[10]

What More is concerned with, therefore, is not the extirpation of sin, although no doubt all good men wish to see that, but a reformation of society which will render certain evils impossible and so eradicate certain kinds of people—the avaricious, the waste-makers, the drones, the impoverished.

For More it was not difficult to conceive of a society which would enable men to live a good life; it would be classless and democratic, although patriarchal. It is of more interest to us today, perhaps, that because Utopia is represented as an existing state it poses all the problems of a socialist state in a non-socialist world. More is centrally concerned here with the manner in which such a state might ensure its survival. He represents the prime duty of the Utopian state as being to protect itself and its people. This it does by using its influence, both economic and diplomatic, to build up a network of friendly buffer states about its frontiers. It seeks to avoid war, but is prepared to wage wars of liberation and wars in alliance with its friends. Wherever possible, however, it seeks to avoid war by sowing discord amongst the ranks of any would-be aggressor or aggressors. Where this fails it has recourse to the employment of mercenaries, then to volunteers, and finally, if its own territory is invaded, to the mobilisation of the whole people. This realistic and rather tough-minded approach to the problems of national defence has upset many of More's liberal critics; they seem happier when they can believe that Utopia is a pious dream—when More shows some appreciation of the practicalities they become uneasy and discomfited.

There are practicalities which create some real difficulties for More—such as how to deal with a population explosion, how malefactors should be punished, how religious toleration could be effected, how aggression should be met—and it may be with these in mind that the More *persona* remarks at the conclusion that he would take issue with certain of the practices of the Utopians. So would we all; few today agree that colonisation is the best solution to the problem of population. But these problems require some kind of solution in the realm of practical politics, and More, or so it seems to me, simply formulates the best that he can conceive and then leaves the matter open for further discussion. It is a matter of idle debate whether at that time any more feasible solutions were available. More's views and opinions, as I have already intimated, are naturally historically limited.

The historical limitations of *Utopia* are quite evident when we consider the discussion of the means by which social evils may be remedied and a better state of social affairs established. This discussion occupies an important place in Book I of *Utopia* and resolves itself into a debate between the More *persona* and Hythloday on the influence which a wise and good man can exert upon a king. The More *persona* is of the opinion that such an adviser might persuade a king to adopt policies of social reformation or, at least, if he is unable to do this, whatever policy decisions were taken could be made less pernicious by his influence. In essence, the More *persona* argues for the social reformist point of view. Hythloday, whom the More *persona* is seeking to persuade to enter upon such a political career, rejects this argument. His view is that the advice of a wise and good counsellor would be politically ineffective and that, far from being able to influence the course of events, his participation in the political process would tend to corrupt him and reduce him to servile opportunism. It is unnecessary to spell out the latter-day relevance of this particular discussion, in which More sets forth the pros and cons of participation from a revolutionary point of view, i.e. from the point of view of one who is concerned with fundamental social change. What should be remarked is the assumption that social change can only be effected from above. Thus it is that in Book II we discover that the constitution of the Utopian state was the work of an enlightened king, King Utopus, after whom the country which he conquered and the state which he established was named.

The general impression left in the mind of the reader of *Utopia* is that the social arrangements are either to be improved from above or they are not going to be improved at all; there is, that is to say, no suggestion that there exists any independent political force outside the establishment. This is the major historical limitation of *Utopia*, for there was in fact, and not simply in More's opinion, no such force. It is true that the merchants and manufacturers were increasing in power and influence, and More himself was closely connected with them, but their position was very much that of the More *persona*. They were becoming a part of the establishment, a pressure group operating through the existing machinery of government, and using the influence afforded by their wealth, rather as do the Utopians in foreign affairs, to ensure that their

B

interests were served. The policies thereby effected were of the kind of which Book I is so critical—the development of the wool trade through enclosures, the monopolisation of trade, the raising of rents and prices.

It should be remarked, to deviate slightly, that with the expansion of trade, which got under way in England towards the end of the fifteenth century, there was a considerable increase in English imports, especially of luxury items such as silks, spices, jewellery and precious metals. To offset the growing volume of imports and maintain the trade balance it was necessary to increase exports. What this meant was that England had to increase the production of its major export, wool.* Hence the spread of the enclosures, as more land was turned over to sheep, and the consequent impoverishment of masses of people which accompanied the great increase in the conspicuous wealth of a minority. Wealth was far more conspicuous than it is today, not because there were fewer rich people and they were very rich, or anything like that, but because the profits of industry were not reinvested, they were accumulated in the form of jewellery, plate and the like. When, at the end of the sixteenth century, the laws against usury were repealed by Parliament and finance capital given a secure footing, profits were invested and the life-style of the English bourgeois became thrifty, plain and puritanical.

The problem of the balance of payments is not a new one and it is interesting to note that in More's day the state was already attempting to manipulate the money market by policies of devaluation and revaluation aimed at redressing the balance of payments:

> First one counselleth to raise and enhance the valuation of money when the king must pay any, and again to call down the value of coin to less than it is worth when he must receive or gather any. For thus great sums shall be paid with a little money, and where little is due much shall be received.[11]

The point I wish to make, however, is that More obviously could not look to the merchants to institute those policies of reform indicated in *Utopia*; he could not expect them to abolish enclosures and thereby destroy the wool trade and with it the export trade and the importation of goods.

Nor could he look to the class which suffered from the policies he

---

* Wool accounted for four-fifths of English exports in the reign of Henry VIII. See Peter Ramsey, *Tudor Economic Problems* (London, 1963), p. 51.

deplores. The peasantry, which had earlier supported such reformers as Wycliffe and John Ball, was disintegrating as a social class; either they were being reduced to a disorganised proletariat, with no means to live but their labour, which being unrequired left them to vagabondage and thievery (as More remarks), or the more fortunate few were becoming independent capitalist farmers producing for the market and consequently having a vested interest in the market and a money economy. These latter were actually merging with the merchants and manufacturers into a distinct class. In these conditions the only effective political force was that of the establishment.* This is understood by More and hence the political choice is seen to lie between attempting to work through the established machinery of government, which is the doctrine of the More *persona*, or of turning one's back upon politics altogether and becoming a drop-out, intent solely upon personal fulfilment, which is the doctrine of Hythloday.

More, then, is centrally concerned with the evils of a society in which the spread of poverty amongst the masses of people is accompanied by the increasing wealth of a few, but he can offer no practical means of social reformation. More, however, was a humanist and as such intent also upon a more limited reformation of life, and in particular upon reforming education and religion. The humanists were so called because they championed the new learning, the humanities, and in particular the study of Greek and the literature of classical antiquity, i.e. the Latin of the classical authors and not that of medieval Europe. This new interest is reflected in Hythloday's account of his discussion with the Utopians:

> When they heard me speak of the Greek literature or learning (for in Latin there was nothing that I thought they would greatly allow, besides historians and poets) they made wonderful earnest and importunate suit unto me that I would teach and instruct them in that tongue and learning.[12]

The second important plank in the humanist programme also gets an honourable mention in the description of Utopian education:

> They be taught learning in their own native tongue. For it is both copious in words and also pleasant to the ear.[13]

Both of these humanist concerns, for the study of Greek and for the use of the vernacular to make knowledge more widely available, become

---

* This is so today in many developing countries; hence the special role of the army in such countries.

essential instruments of the Protestant Reformation. The knowledge of Greek produced a means of returning to the Gospels at source, avoiding the medieval accretions, whilst the campaign for the vernacular provided the driving force for the production of the vernacular Bible, which made the word of God directly available to every literate individual—even if it did transform the Word that was flesh into one that was ink and paper. It is ironic that of all the policies outlined in *Utopia* those which were to be implemented in More's own time are precisely those which unleashed the reformation More consistently resisted, the Protestant Reformation. That other reformation, which would eradicate the wastemakers and the impoverished, was to remain a pious dream. A revolution was soon to get under way in England, but it was to be one which was to lead to the coronation of Lady Money, the story of whose ascension is best told in the love poetry of the sixteenth century.

Love Poetry in the Sixteenth Century

I. THE COMING OF THE GOLDEN AGE

I once reached the general conclusion in a discussion of the poetry of
Sir Thomas Wyatt and his contemporaries that a new and more
ornamental conception of poetry emerged in the second half of the
sixteenth century.[1] There was, or so it seemed to me at the time, a
highly self-conscious emphasis upon superficialities at the expense of
substance in the general run of Elizabethan poetry, something which,
in the words of Sir Philip Sidney, did "bewray a want of inward
tuch", suggesting an attenuation of present experience and a loss of
contact with the past, especially with those ranges of experience which
made courtly love and the ideals of chivalry something more than *mere*
conventions. However, later consideration has led me to believe that
this was a wrong way of putting the matter and to prefer the final
judgement of my essay, which was that "courtly love and chivalry are
already things of the past in the Elizabethan period. . . . But courtly
love and chivalry are not isolated phenomena; they are aspects of a
much wider and more general manner of evaluating and expressing
the relationships of men and women, to each other, to the world in
which they live, and to God, all of which were undergoing a radical, if
not revolutionary, change in the sixteenth century."[2]

One indication of this change is the rise of new idioms which testify
to new habits of appraisal and to new visions of social life. Of these the
ones which are of particular importance in the sixteenth century, in
that they promote new conceptions of human nature, are those which
express personal affections in economic terms. A modern American
instance of such a metamorphosis is that from "I very much like the
look of her" to "She looks like a million dollars." As the social experience of North America, crystallised in the idioms of its language, com-
mits its lovers to a business-like rôle, Wyatt's love poems were constrained by the social conventions of his time as these were represented
in the feudal idioms of courtly love.

The strength of this constraining influence may explain why many of the poems currently ascribed to Wyatt are anonymous in style. Poems such as "The hart and servys to yow profferd", "And wylt thow leve me thus", "As power and wytt wyll me Assyst", "Howe shulde I", and many others in the Devonshire manuscript, are conventional poems of courtly love which any of his contemporaries and immediate predecessors could equally well have written. The emergence of the strong personality of "The longe love", "Who so list to hount", "It may be good", "They fle from me", and other poems, from the prevailing anonymity, can be accounted for by seeing Wyatt's poetry as the attempt of an increasingly self-conscious individual to establish his own identity within the conventions of his time. His profound unease and dissatisfaction arises from the conventional, or idiomatic, compulsion to translate his emotional responses into political terms and so alienate his personal need for honest, reciprocal affection. His poetry, in other words, is an illustration of the clash between a desperate personal need and the impersonal and ceremonial forms which such needs assumed in the Court of Henry VIII.

The degree of consciousness which makes such a clash possible suggests, of course, that Wyatt was peculiarly sensitive, but a condition of such a degree of sensitivity is a general weakening and questioning of the social conventions and of the power these exercise over conduct and opinion. The cultural implications of humanism, the decimation of the old nobility and the attack upon the old religious establishment are indications rather than causes of the social upheaval that was taking place in the early decades of the sixteenth century. That there was something rotten in the state of England was generally recognised; More provided a lucid account of contemporary social ills in *Utopia* and Thomas Starkey offered the following diagnosis:

Like as in a dropsy the body is unwieldy unlusty and slow, nothing quick to move, nother apt nor meet for any manner of exercise but swollen with ill humours, lieth idle and unprofitable to all outward labour, so is a commonalty replenished with negligent and idle people, unlusty and unwieldy nothing quick in the exercise of arts and crafts whereby her wealth should be maintained and supported, but swollen with such ill humours, boileth out with all vice, mischief and misery, the which out of idelness (as out of a fountain) issueth and springeth. This is the mother of many other sickness and grievous diseases in our politic body, and the greatest destruction of the common weal therein that may be devised.[3]

The extent to which the old order of things was collapsing in early Tudor England is detailed for us by More in the first book of *Utopia* and by Starkey in the course of his dialogue. In its place a new order was emerging, acidly described by More as "a certain conspiracy of rich men procuring their own commodities under the name and title of the commonwealth", who "invent and devise all means and crafts, first how to keep safely, without fear of losing, that they have unjustly gathered together, and next how to hire and abuse the work and labour of the poor for as little money as may be. These devices, when the rich men have decreed to be kept and observed under colour of the commonalty, that is to say, also of the poor people, then they be made laws."*

Bearing in mind the social disintegration recorded by More and Starkey, it is plainly not by accident that Wyatt's poetry at its best is pervaded by feelings of nostalgia at the sacrifice of old conventions and the securities of sophisticated communal feeling these represented; nor, consequently, is it accidental that such a sacrifice should give to the lover in Wyatt's poems such a dramatic insecurity. Wyatt's search for assurance is significantly an appeal against conventional feeling to that which is 'within', to the real state of the affections. It is this characteristic of his best work that has led to the claim that he introduced the introspective note into English poetry. The caving-in of the habitual modes of life left the individual adrift in an ethically chaotic world and, critical of what was taking place about him, he was forced to search within himself for the materials out of which to construct some sound discipline of life.

It was this moment of social collapse, so well recorded by More, Starkey and Wyatt in their different ways, that sponsored the Renaissance interest in man and made Protestantism appear spiritually significant by making it conceivable that a reformation of life could take place around the inner conviction of the enlightened individual.† In a society still possessing a strong code of opinion and conduct such a conception would have seemed merely eccentric.

Protestantism was fashioned, as all other areas of human awareness were being fashioned, by new norms expressed in new idioms. In the

---

* More, pp. 132–3. This is probably the first expression of the conspiratorial theory of the ruling class. Although sociologically primitive, this theory enables More to grasp the class basis of law and to understand the rôle of the ruling class as the promulgator of legal fictions.

† This belief gives special relevance to More's discussion, in *Utopia*, of the political effectiveness of the enlightened individual as an instrument of social reform.

course of the sixteenth century these cease to be feudal, that is political (those of service, duty, etc.) and become economic (those of buying, selling, etc.) and with the affections thus abstracted to economic objects and relations instead of to political persons and affiliations, we have the establishment of that most conclusive alienation of the emotional life, the increasing omnipotence of money.

It is the peculiar virtue of money to shut off the sensibilities from the natural objects of the affections—as in the idiom of American capitalism a million dollars interposes its attractions between appreciative male and lovely female. More was quick to realise this; the feudal lady had given place to 'Lady Money' (the "common whore of mankind", as Shakespeare ungallantly calls her) who had come to "stop up the way between us and our living". "Money", as D. H. Lawrence remarked four centuries later, "is like walls between us, we are immured in gold, and we die of starvation or etiolation."[4] It is this starvation or etiolation of the affectional life which gives the impression that much Elizabethan poetry lacks substance and it is a built-in feature of the new outlook that was taking shape in England during Elizabeth's reign.

This new outlook was remarked upon by Thomas Whythorne in the 1570's. Writing in his autobiography of the attitude adopted by his contemporaries in appraising each other, he complains that

> A great number thez daies do meaziur honesty by welth. az if thei praiz A rich man thei will sai he iz an honest man, I warrant him hee iz wurth somuch (and then thei will nam [A] sum). lykwyz if thei dispyz or dispraiz A poor man, thei will sai that hee iz but A beggerly knav, and not worth A grot. and so akkording to the quantite of a mans substans thei will akkownt him honest, and so to bee kredited and beleeved.[5]

What in fact Whythorne was deploring are the idioms to which a money-economy automatically gives rise. Against such evaluations he voices the traditional objection that the right distinction between man and man, that which obtains in the eyes of God, is not one that can be made by wealth and the language of wealth, and therefore that

> thei ar far wyd from the mark who hav such affyans in welth and riches and thei ar to bee suspekted that either thei know not what thei say when thei do say so, or els thei ar to bee thouht that all their honestiez lieth in their welth. and tharfor thei do somuch extoll rich folk for their riches sak withowt dew konsiderasion thereof, or of sender and giver therof.[6]

The new idioms and dispositions, against which Whythorne inveighs, were created by the changing values of human association, values which find their reflection in a new imagery, expressing in an ideal or 'poetic' form the real nature of man's relationship to man—and more importantly to woman—in the new society.

The emergence of a new norm, expressed in a new idiom and attended by a correspondingly new conception of individual substance and style, is evident in the love poetry of the sixteenth century. This poetry is of particular relevance to an understanding of the human community in Elizabethan England (as it is to that of the early-Tudor Court) because, as has frequently been acknowledged, the relation of the sexes is our most important clue to the level of human development achieved in any particular society. As Thorstein Veblen, perhaps the greatest and certainly the most entertaining of America's sociologists, remarked towards the end of the last century,

> It has been well and repeatedly said by popular writers and speakers who reflect the common sense of intelligent people on questions of social structure and function that the position of woman in any community is the most striking index of the level of culture attained by the community, and it might be added, by any given class in the community.[7]

Probably the popular writers and speakers Veblen refers to were those Boston feminists Henry James treats with such male arrogance in his novel *The Bostonians*. The opinion which Veblen recommends (and which neatly places James's "level of culture") had been earlier expressed by Marx—

> The direct, natural, and necessary relation of person to person is the relation of man to woman. . . . From this relationship one can therefore judge man's whole level of development[8]

—and was reiterated later by D. H. Lawrence when he declared that

> The great relationship, for humanity, will always be the relation between men and women. The relation between man and man, woman and woman, parent and child, will always be subsidiary.
> And the relation between man and woman will change for ever, and will for ever be the new central clue to human life.[9]

It is an opinion which receives its classic formulation in Lawrence's novel, *The Rainbow*.

Like Beauty, Truth and Justice, Love is an abstraction and has seldom been more than a figure of speech in the relations of the sexes. That love "has no great influence upon the sum of life"[10] is an opinion which Dr. Johnson shared with the poets of Greek antiquity, "not one in all the multitude" of whom, according to Phaedrus, had "ever composed a single panegyric of so ancient and mighty a god as Love".[11] No doubt to an age conditioned by the lyricists of Denmark Street to believe that love makes the world go round such neglect of a fundamental passion is hardly credible. This incredulity, however, gives particular expression to one of the most unreflective and unhistorical of all commonplaces, the belief that whilst civilisations come and go, love, hate, despair, hope, joy, sorrow, and similar abstractions, provide the unchanging stuff of human emotional experience. Such a belief is fatally wounded by the observation that the emotional ties which bind people together in a feudal world are substantially different from those prevailing in our own society. The difference is well marked in the poetry of the sixteenth century, the century in which England moved decisively out of the feudal and into the modern world.

During the first half of the sixteenth century English poets are still almost exclusively aware of love as a feudal bond, as a form of feudal service; indeed, they more commonly offer a lady service than love. The function of the conceit in Wyatt's "The longe love" (a 'translation' from Petrarch) is to establish love as the lover's lord and to define love as a natural feudal obligation.

> The longe love, that in my thought doeth harbar,
> And in myn hert doth kepe his residence,
> Into my face preseth with bold pretence,
> And therin campeth, spreding his baner.
> She that me lerneth to love and suffre
> And will that my trust, and lustes negligence
> Be rayned by reason, shame, and reverence
> With his hardines taketh displeasure.
> Wherewithall, unto the hertes forrest he fleith,
> Leving his entreprise with payne and cry
> And there him hideth and not appereth.
> What may I do when my maister fereth,
> But, in the felde, with him to lyve and dye?
> For goode is the liff, ending faithfully. (IV)

The "hertes forrest" into which the lover follows his defeated lord symbolises not only the naturalness of the heart's affections, but also the apparent naturalness of the feudal bond between the servant and his lord (his 'natural' superior). It is only by following his lord that the servant-lover can realise the naturalness of his affections and envision a life well spent: "For goode is the liff, ending faithfully", as the poem concludes.

The definition of love as service is further typified in the opening lines of one of Wyatt's original poems:

> My hert I gave the not to do it payn,
>   But to preserue it was to the taken;
>   I serued the not to be forsaken,
>   But that I should be rewarded again.
> I was content thy seruant to remayn,
>   But not to be payed vnder this fasshion. (XIV)

Such a complaint has its justification in the feudal doctrine of reciprocal duties; the bond of obligation between servant and lord (or lady) was a mutual one and it is this bond which the lady is felt to have broken. In brief, Wyatt's feelings for his lady are those of a feudal vassal for his feudal lord or liege lady. When such a poet refers to himself as his lady's thrall it is not simply a polite or literary affectation but a reflection of a socially meaningful relationship.

The suggestion in the final line of the above stanza, that the lover expected "to be payed", may lead a modern reader to presume that Wyatt finally presents the servant as a wage-labourer rather than as a vassal, as Sidney does later in the century when he observes that

> Dearely the servants doo their wages buy,
> Revil'd for ech small fault. . . .[12]

At the time Wyatt was writing, however, capitalism had not yet transubstantiated the language of human relationships; *payment* had the sense of *satisfaction* and it was literally true that "He is well paid that is well satisfied." This was no longer so when Shakespeare was thus defining Portia's satisfaction in *The Merchant of Venice* (IV.i.411) and supporting her use of *paid* with the ironic confession, "My mind was never yet more mercenary" (IV.i.414).

That *payment* was no longer ordinarily used in such a way by the time of Shakespeare is some indication of the changes in language, and consequently in outlook, which had occurred during the sixteenth century. A similar alteration was taking place in the use of a whole family of words; words and phrases were being stripped of their feudal significance and assuming the more impersonal meaning appropriate to a world of commercial transactions.★

The bulk of Wyatt's poems, and those of the new company of courtly makers to which he belonged, still appraise the affections in the language of feudalism. This is not to say, of course, that other kinds of appraisal were not being made; a man would seek to procure his lady's favour by service, but he would also put her in remembrance of him by presenting her with some costly trinket. In one of Wyatt's poems the lover offers his heart to his lady in place of a jewel because, as he explains,

> I cannot gyve browches nor Ringes,
> These goldsmythes work and goodly thinges,
> Piery nor perle oryente and clere. (LXXXV)

The world in which Wyatt's poetry has its roots is one in which wealth is felt to count for something, although in general it serves only to give emphasis to distinctions of degree, as may be gathered from the concluding lines of "Who so list to hount":

> And graven with Diamondes in letters plain
> There is written her faier neck rounde abowte:
> "Noli me tangere for Cesars I ame,
> And wylde for to hold though I seme tame." (VII)

The diamonds here, although symbolic of wealth, are only instrumental in defining the claims of Caesar's (the King's) ownership; the warning is not "Don't touch me because I am expensive" but "Don't touch me because I am the King's".

In general, pre-Elizabethan poetry bears witness to the fact that the heart's affections were felt to be as natural and as unchanging as feudal bondage. Although Wyatt's poetry expresses a pathetic sense of the inadequacies of this presumption, it is still largely constrained by it. "Who so list to hount", for example, alludes to the untouchability of

---

★ For Wyatt, for instance, *fee* still meant *an estate held by homage*; *in fee* meant *subject to feudal obligation*; *fynaunce* meant *to take as ransom*; *mortgage* meant *security*; *price* meant *estimation*; *a purchase* meant *an endeavour*; *thrift* meant *luck*; *commodity* meant *advantage*. These assumed their modern meanings in the course of the sixteenth century. During the same period *merchant* began to be used in the same way as our *chap* (see Ernest Weekley, *The Romance of Words*, Guild Books No. 407, London, 1949, p. 57) which is itself an abbreviation of *chapman*, i.e. merchant. Similar changes were taking place in other departments of the language. Engels remarked that English law retained "in the main the forms of the old feudal laws while giving them a bourgeois content; in fact, directly giving a bourgeois meaning to the old feudal name" (*Ludwig Feuerbach and the Outcome of Classical German Philosophy*, ed. C. P. Dutt (London, n.d.), p. 63).

Caesar's wife in a line—"Noli me tangere for Cesars I ame"—which, whilst rendering the Latin motto *Noli me tangere quia Caesaris sum*, relies for its irony upon Christ's use of the phrase *Noli me tangere* ("Touch me not for I am not yet ascended unto the Father," John xx. 17) and his command that we should render unto Caesar the things that are Caesar's and unto God the things that are God's (Matthew xxii. 21). By conflating these two commands the motto convicts the lady (thought by some to have been Anne Boleyn) of rendering unto Caesar the things that are God's. Thus, whilst recognising the royal prerogative, Wyatt creates an awareness of a higher allegiance and so feeds into his poem a sense of the inadequacy of an affectional tie sanctioned by degree alone. Nevertheless, this sense of inadequacy is only surreptitiously at work behind an overt acceptance of the claims of degree.

The old feudal idioms do not die overnight, of course, but continue in use throughout the sixteenth century. Turberville, Watson, Greene, Raleigh, Davies of Hereford, Munday, Campion and Shakespeare cast their lovers variously in the rôles of servant, vassal and thrall, rôles commonly assumed by lovers in Elizabethan anthologies. But these are already felt as poetic extravagancies and old-world gallantries. Feudal idioms wither away, and with them the poetry of courtly love, although some terms of feudal love enter the more permanent vocabulary of the language: *enthrall*, *service* and *duty* no longer have their feudal significance and although, as late as 1594, Richard Barnfield could argue in *The Shepheards*, that "He is a Courtier, for he courts his Loue", *to court* and *courtship* had already ceased to be peculiar to the Court and to courtly love.

The decline of courtly love poetry seems to date from the death of Wyatt in 1542. The wider relationship of that date to the decline of the courtly way of life is indicated by Tawney:

> Into commerce, industry and agriculture alike, the revolution in prices,* gradual for the first third of the century, but after 1540 a mill race, injected a virus of hitherto unsuspected potency, at once a stimulant to feverish enterprise and an acid dissolving all customary relationships.[13]

---

* Some measure of the revolution in prices which took place in the 1540's is provided by R. B. Outhwaite, *Inflation in Tudor and Early Stuart England*, Studies in Economic History, ed. M. W. Flinn (London, 1969), p. 13: "Once underway . . . inflation proceeded rapidly. This is particularly true of agricultural prices, which reached, by the 1550's, an average level . . . 95 per cent above that of the 1530's. Industrial prices rose more slowly, but even so they were in the 1550's some 70 per cent above those ruling in the 1530's."

Elizabethan poetry, by and large, is commanded by idioms which express the new patterns of social life, its new ideals and attitudes. By 1550 John Harington, in "A Sonnet made on Isabella Markham", had succeeded in emancipating his love from the feudal constraints which chafed Wyatt. To the question "Whence comes my love?" Harington could reply,

> From lips that spoil the ruby's praise,
> From eyes that mock the diamond's blaze.[14]

Pope believed that

> Though the same sun with all diffusive rays
> Blush in the rose and in the diamond blaze,
> We prize the stronger effort of his power
> And justly set the gem above the flower.
>
> (*Epistle to Cobham*, lines 97–100)

But Pope is being naïve. Harington's reference to the ruby and the diamond brings into play a quality of excellence denied to the blushing rose and the blazing sun.* His love for Isabella derives from a beauty the distinctive quality of which is its superlative expensiveness; gems may be allowed a sensuous beauty, but "their rarity and price adds an expression of distinction to them, which they would never have if they were cheap".[15] When Elizabethan poets, such as Morley, Shakespeare, Skoloker and Sylvester, refer to the lady as a jewel they are using an idiom (still current) which endears the lady by a surreptitious appeal to the criterion of expensiveness.[16] It is the presence of the kind of awareness marked by such an idiom that makes the poetry of Sir Philip Sidney so radically different from that of Wyatt and his fellows.

In reading the poetry of Sidney we are in contact with a world in which axioms of taste and behaviour are modern rather than feudal, a world in which material wealth, although "not commonly present, consciously, in our canons of taste . . . is none the less present as a constraining norm, selectively shaping and sustaining our sense of what

---

* If diamonds and rubies suggested themselves as comparisons more readily to Harington than they would have done to a poet of an earlier generation this was in part due to the fact that they had become a commoner and more obtrusive sight than they had been. About the time Harington was writing his sonnet, the doctor in Sir Thomas Smith's *Discourse of the Common Weal* was remarking upon "the great store and plenty of treasure, which is walking in these parts of the world, far more in these our dayes, than ever our forefathers have seen in times past" (E. Lamond, ed., *A Discourse of the Common Weal of this Realm of England*, Cambridge, 1893, p. 187). The doctor explains this phenomenon as the result of the new trade with the Indies.

is beautiful, and guiding our discrimination with respect to what may
be legitimately approved as beautiful and what may not".[17] The
approbation bestowed by riches is not limited, however, to the beauties
of outward form, it also characterises the social and spiritual virtues.
Sidney's Stella is not merely "Rich in all beauties which man's eye can
see", but also

> Rich in the treasure of deserv'd renowne,
> Rich in the riches of a royall hart,
> Rich in those gifts which give the eternall crowne.[18]

Sidney's devotion to the beauties of Lady Rich—"rich, naming my
Stella's name"[19]—is itself a metaphor of this newly predominant condition of human awareness.

Sidney was not unaware of this condition of his, or at least Astrophil's, nature* and in one poem confessed himself to be

> In nature apt to like when I did see
> Beauties, which were of manie Carrets fine.[20]

And that aptness, or rather aptitude, "selectively shaping and sustaining
our sense of what is beautiful" as we read through Sidney, is present in
his appraisals of Stella, of her appearance and her virtues. A succinct
illustration of this is provided by the ninth sonnet of the *Astrophil and
Stella* sequence:

> Queene *Vertue's* court, which some call *Stella's* face,
>   Prepar'd by Nature's chiefest furniture,
>   Hath his front built of Alabaster pure;
> Gold is the covering of that stately place.
> The doore by which sometimes comes forth her Grace,
>   Red Porphir is, which locke of pearle makes sure:
>   Whose porches rich (which name of cheekes endure)
> Marble mixt red and white do enterlace.
> The windowes now through which this heav'nly guest
> Looks over the world, and can find nothing such,
> Which dare claime from those lights the name of best,
>   Of touch they are that without touch doth touch,
>   Which *Cupid's* selfe from Beautie's myne did draw:
>   Of touch they are, and poore I am their straw.

---

* It should be noted that in the following lines *nature* refers to the inherent tendencies of
Astrophil and not the material world and in the next sonnet, "Queene *Vertue's* court",
front has the added Latin sense of 'forehead'.

It would appear from this eulogy that Stella's face is her fortune, for her beauties are certainly "of manie Carrets fine". One is initially tempted to remark that Sidney fails to keep his eye upon the object and to concede Rosemond Tuve's claim that "not even the schoolboy of the sixteenth century is told to keep his eye on the object".[21] That, however, would be to mistake the object of Sidney's real attention, which is not a lady's face but a rich and sumptuous palace, one of those enchanted palaces of the poets which Bacon advises builders not to copy in his essay *Of Building*.* Stella is actually viewed with much the same appreciation as Elizabethan tourists displayed for the architecture of Italy; on the whole it is "vulgar, admiring a work in terms of its materials, exclaiming at a profusion of gold leaf, pricing rare marbles, and exclaiming at ingenuity".[22] Nor would it do to overlook the implication, slight though it may be, that the values with which the poem is centrally concerned are superior to those of mere flesh and blood, that the "porches rich" have to *endure* the "name of cheekes". Such is the endurance imposed upon the love of riches by the demands of amorous compliment. The mind's eye is dazzled in this sonnet, then, not by the beauty and virtue of Stella, but by a lavish display of wealth; wealth is used variously to define purity, stateliness, beauty and virtue, and so, as far as Stella is concerned, to alienate the lover's affections. And if this suggests that Sidney's muse is Mammon, it is a suggestion tacitly accepted by Astrophil when (in sonnet 32) he asks, of his superlatively expensive lady,

> Whence hast thou Ivorie, Rubies, pearle and gold,
> To shew her skin, lips, teeth and head so well?

Not surprisingly, Morpheus, the Muse addressed, is unable to reply to this misdirected query. As will appear later, Sidney was not the only Elizabethan poet in whose conceit love gave rise to dreams of unaccountable riches.

"Queene *Vertue*'s court" was obviously intended as a compliment, but as Izaak Walton remarked in his *Life of Donne*, "wealth hath seldom been the Portion, and never the Mark to discover good People", and Sidney's sonnet does nothing to falsify that judgement. At a serious level, then, it is open to an objection, which may be summed up in the words of Thomas Whythorne:

* And, in reply to Miss Tuve, it needs to be remarked that it was Francis Bacon, an ex-Elizabethan schoolboy, who observed in sect. 6 of the plan of *The Great Instauration* that "all depends upon keeping the eye fixed upon the facts of nature and so receiving their images simply as they are".

Az A golden brydell, althouh it garnish A hors, it maketh him never the better, so althouh riches do garnish A man, yet kan thei not mak him good, wher riches ar honored, good men ar dispyzed.[23]

In this sense Sidney can be said to have 'dispyzed', or at least to have disprized, Stella. I am not suggesting that this was Sidney's intention; the point of the poem is not to establish that Stella is an expensive luxury, although this is the achieved result.

Indeed the reader might well complain, with an anonymous contributor to *A Handful of Pleasant Delights* (1584), that in Elizabethan love poetry

> The gravers of the golden shows
> With jewels do beset me,

since that to prove how dearly he loves his lady the Elizabethan poet

> With pearles and rubyes makes her monuments.[24]

Sir John Davies, in the seventh of his *Hymns to Astraea*, praises Queen Elizabeth to other ladies:

> Excellent jewels would you see?
> Lovely ladies! Come with me!
> I will (for love I owe you)
> Shew you as rich a treasury
> As East or West can shew you!

It is tempting to suppose that Davies has been distracted by the gold-embroidered, jewel-spangled gowns the Queen was given to wearing, which are so well depicted in Hillyard's well-known portrait of her. It seems more likely, however, that the bejewelled and gilded images of the Virgin, recently plundered from the Churches, found their permanent memorial in the work of poets who called them to mind when treating their ladies as things enshrined and sainted. For it isn't, as we've seen from "Queene *Vertue*'s court", only the Queen who is represented so affluently. Drummond's Alexis spreads

> the treasure of her hair
> More rich than that brought from Colchian mines;

lines which place Drummond along with Sidney (notice the reference to 'Beautie's myne' in "Queen *Vertue*'s court") and Donne (in "Elegy XIX, To His Mistress Going to Bed") as the kind of poet Rankins satirises as

c

> In songs and sonnets taking such a grace,
> As if he delu'd for gold in Indian mines.

John Lyly's Daphne also has hair which is "twisted gold" and, not to be outdone, Greene's Samela not only has "her tresses gold", but "Her teeth are pearl" and her "breasts are ivory". Lodge's Rosalind has eyes which are "sapphires set in snow" and

> With orient pearl, with ruby red,
> With marble white, with sapphires blue,
> Her body every way is fed.

William Warner's mistress has "a body white as ivory" and John Marston's is also a

> Delicious beauty, that doth lie
> Wrapped in a skin of ivory.

When William Drummond dreams of love it is of

> The ivory, coral, gold,
> Of breast, of lips, of hair.[25]

Whilst to Spenser "Woman is like a stately merchant ship which brings to her husband riches and credit."* His lady-love is therefore

> Fayre when her brest lyke a rich laden barke,
> with pretious merchandise she forth doth lay

and

> fayrest she, when so she doth display
> the gate with pearles and rubyes richly dight
> throgh which her words so wise do make their way,

whilst in his *Epithalamion*

> Her long loose yellow locks lyke golden wyre,
> Sprinckled with perle, and perling flowres a tweene,
> Do lyke a golden mantle her attyre.[26]

The unpleasant tactile suggestion of hair like wire is, of course, accidental; the imagery of conspicuous wealth is essentially visual. This particular image is not an uncommon one: Shakespeare, in Sonnet 30, remarks of his Dark Lady that "If hairs be wires, black wires grow on

---

* Louis B. Wright suggests that William Austin, *Haec Homo* (1637), "is probably quoting this figure from a marriage sermon by Robert Wilkinson, published in 1607 as *The Merchant Royal (Middle-Class Culture in Elizabethan England*, 1958, p. 503 and n.). Wilkinson may well have taken the figure from Spenser.

her head"; Wotton "In Praise of his Daphnis", in *England's Helicon* (1600), writes that "Her tresses are like wires of beaten gold" and in Barnfield's *The Affectionate Shepheard* (1594) the shepherd bids his love, "Cut off thy locke, and sell it for gold wier".

It would be tedious to prolong this catalogue of love's new treasure trove; it serves to indicate the extent to which Sidney's sonnet "Queene *Vertue*'s court" typifies the decorousness of Elizabethan love poetry. The examples quoted are commonplace enough to offer a fair idea of the constraint which holds Sidney's "young braine captiv'd in golden cage", a constraint which is admirably, if unwittingly recognised by Dyer's Coridon when he refers to his lady as "the golden fetter of my mind" and which Pilkington set to music in a madrigal:

> Have I found her? O rich finding!
> Goddess-like for to behold,
> Her fair tresses seemly binding
> In a chain of pearl and gold.
> Chain me, chain me, O most fair,
> Chain me to thee with that hair![27]

Thus, whilst the Elizabethan poets may be a nest of singing birds, one can not help feeling, with Pilkington and those two friends Sidney and Dyer, that (as Wyatt had acidly remarked of court life)

> who so ioyes such kinde of life to holde,
> In prison ioyes, fettred with cheines of gold.
>   (CCLIX)

2. PUTTING ON THE STYLE

> *But who so thinkes the signe the substance is,*
> *Erres, and his wit doth wander much amisse.*
>   William Rankins.

As a complimentary poem providing an inventory of the lady's praiseworthy qualities, Sidney's "Queen *Vertue*'s court" might well be called a traditional love poem. Wyatt and his fellows were perfectly familiar with the genre and adept at the art of amorous compliment. But it is notable that the lover's attachment to his lady in early Tudor court poetry has little to do with the lady's personal qualities; her physical features are rarely mentioned and she may be generous or mean, kind or cruel, 'tame' or 'dangerous'. All this is of little moment to the lover's basic attachment because, as he so often points out, he is bound to serve her:

to Reffrayne yt passythe my might:
Wherfor to serue and suffer styll I must.[1]

His situation is that of the feudal vassal, tied to his lord irrespective of his lord's character. If his lord is a bad master, he must be content "to serue and suffer" and pray for better times. The vassal, after all, is not a free moral agent; he does not serve his lord because he believes his lord is worthy but because his lord is his 'natural' superior. It would be pointless, therefore, to argue with the courtly lover that his lady is not worth serving, or to suggest that he would never serve such a creature were he not unhinged by love, since such contentions ignore the feudal implications of 'service'.

Whilst "Queen *Vertue*'s court" may be described as a traditional love poem its dispositions are not those of courtly love. It is true that Stella's superiority is presented as natural, but her natural superiority turns out to be indistinguishable from mere expensiveness. This is the essence of Sidney's compliment; it not only presents Stella's virtues as costly but provides a detailed appreciation of her physical features as costly *furnishings*. What we have in Sidney's sonnet, then, is an instance of the operation of a constraining norm, "the golden fetter", making itself further and more subtly felt in an equation between style and ornamentation, the norm of material wealth having its correspondence in a style which is richly decorative. It is this correspondence between the pervasive norm and the prevailing style in Elizabethan love poetry which constitutes its decorum. It is not fortuitous that Sidney, like Spenser, and Shakespeare in the Sonnets, frequently refers to what he is about in terms of painting, gilding, enamelling and adorning. What is so consistently revealed in these idioms is a richly ornamental concern for poetic form.

Miss Tuve believes that

> We have seen in the earlier [i.e. Elizabethan] poets a decorative diction and an unfunctional use of sensuous images for pure exuberance of ornamentation, and have seen them as evidence of barriers erected between the poet and reality.[2]

In this view, Miss Tuve argues, 'we' have been wrong. Certainly, the opinion that the ornament and decoration in Elizabethan poetry erects a barrier between the poet and reality is mistaken, because it does not recognise the evident connection between the poetry and the reality of conspicuous wealth. However, there is no doubt that the Elizabethan poets did indulge in decorative diction and an exuberance of ornamentation and did so by design, as George Puttenham makes quite plain. According to Puttenham it is form which distinguishes a true courtly poet and therefore, he argues, if you wish to become a courtly poet you must learn to decorate your poetry in the proper manner. And so he sets himself the task of itemising and explaining a large variety of rhetorical devices, or figures, as he calls them, that should be used by way of decoration. Poetry, he maintains at one point, is like a lady of the Court, most attractive when most expensively attired:

> as we see in these great Madames of honour, be they for personage or otherwise neuer so comely and bewtifull, yet if they want their courtly habillements or at leastwise such other apparell as custome and ciuilitie haue ordained to couer their naked bodies, would be halfe ashamed or greatly out of countenance to be seen in that sort, and perchance do then thinke themselues more amiable in euery mans eye, when they be in their richest attire, suppose of silkes or tyssewes and costly embroderies, then when they go in cloth or in any other plaine and simple apparell. Even so cannot our vulgar Poesie shew it selfe either gallant or gorgious, if any lymme be left naked and bare and not clad in his kindly clothes and coulours, such as may conuey them somwhat out of sight, that is from the common course of ordinary speech and capacities of the vulgar iudgement, and yet being artificially handled must needes yeld it much more bewtie and commendation. This ornament we speak of is giuen to it by figures and figuratiue speaches, which be the flowers as it were and colours that a Poet setteth vpon his language by arte, as the embroderer doth his stone and perle, or passements of gold vpon the stuffe of a Princely garment, or as th'excellent painter bestoweth the rich Orient coulours vpon his table of pourtraite.[3]

It is not difficult to see how, in this passage, the mystique of conspicuous wealth promotes a conception of style as adornment.* When Puttenham compares style to the gowns of Court ladies he is not merely expressing a conviction that it should be sumptuous, he is also expressing

* Rosemond Tuve has urged that it is wrong to dismiss the imagery and rhetoric of Elizabethan poetry as mere ornamentation; she points to the 'craftmanship' involved and the extent to which the poet was still considered a maker. However, the embroiderer is also a craftsman and ornamentation can be profoundly significant without ceasing to be ornamentation. Furthermore, despite Miss Tuve's argument, the Elizabethans themselves usually refer to style as a garment set off by images and rhetorical figures. The passage quoted from Puttenham is certainly more representative of the critical idiom of the times than the sentence quoted by Miss Tuve (*op. cit.*, p. 29) in which he speaks of figurative speeches as a means of polishing the language and "fashioning it to this or that *measure and proportion*".

his sense of it as something which is put on, as a fashion-conscious woman puts on a fashionable dress because she believes it improves her appearance and makes her "more amiable in euery mans eye". What Puttenham is saying is that poets should treat their verses as the ladies of the Court treat their naked bodies, "be they for personage or otherwise neuer so comely and bewtifull". The implications of this view of style may be seen in Spenser's *Shepheardes Calendar* when the verses appeal to the fashion for Chaucer and for courtly love.

In Spenser's early years Chaucer was in high repute; "the fine courtier", Thomas Wilson remarked in his *Art of Rhetoric* (1553) "wil talke nothyng but Chaucer".[4] It was natural that the aspiring young poet should emulate the fashionable old master, Tityrus as he is called in *The Shepheardes Calendar*, where Spenser acknowledges him rather fatuously as "the God of shepherds" and, more truly, as the poet "who taught me homely, as I can, to make".[5] At times Spenser's recollection of Chaucer amounts almost to parody, as in the following passage from the May Aeglogue:

> Sicker this morrowe, ne lenger agoe,
> I sawe a shole of shepheardes outgoe,
> With singing, and shoulting, and iolly chere:
> Before them yode a lusty Tabrere,
> That to the many a Horne pype playd,
> Whereto they dauncen eche one with his mayd.
> To see those folkes make such iouysaunce,
> Made my heart after the pype to daunce.
> Tho to the greene Wood they speeden hem all,
> To fetchen home May with their musicall . . .

This is as competent as much of the pseudo-Chaucer that found its way into sixteenth-century editions; it is remarkable only as a clear demonstration that Chaucer, the fount of the courtly tradition in our literature, had become archaic by the time Spenser is writing. What Spenser is unable to realise are the habits of thought and feeling which inform Chaucer's English. I am thinking in particular of the ease with which the aristocratic, the learned and the vulgar—or in other terms, the courtly, the allegoric and the racily idiomatic—collaborate to give his poetry its vivid and multilateral sociability. In this Chaucer's language reflects that communality of interests which made the relationship of the various strata of medieval English society something more than a merely economic one. And it is precisely the values of Chaucer's language, as an intimate expression of medieval habits of social living, that Spenser's imitation fails to create. Nor is this very surprising, of course, when one considers the great changes that had taken place in social life during the hundred-and-eighty odd years that separated Spenser from Chaucer. In imitating Chaucer Spenser's language is no more adequate to the life of Elizabethan England than that of Wordsworth would be to the times in which we now live. It is perhaps in terms of this inadequacy that Ben Jonson's criticism of Spenser, that in "affecting the Ancients [he] writ no Language", can best be understood. Coming to Chaucer too soon, Jonson maintains, poets fail to apprehend his weightiness and so become "barren in language".[6]

Spenser's Chaucerisms also provide an instance of Elizabethan imitation. Since they do not spring expressively from Elizabethan life what they involve is a matter of appearance. By their use Spenser's poetry is given the appearance of the older poetry of which Chaucer was the recognized master, just as new courtiers give their writings an appearance of courtliness by following the dictates of Puttenham and using certain devices which can be learnt off by heart. Pietro Bembo set out a similar programme for the Italians, a "doctrine of imitation applied to the vernacular: Italians who wished to write well should write with the style of Boccaccio and of Petrarch . . . prose like Boccaccio's, verse like Petrarch's."[7]

In *The Shepheardes Calendar* the most obviously courtly device is the lover's complaint. Spenser's handling of this is more indicative of his relationship to the old courtly conventions than any other single aspect of his poetry. The conventions of courtly love, to which of course the lover's complaint belongs, are more peculiarly courtly than any other convention of the courtly tradition. Allegory and fable, for example, although they are naturally employed by courtly poets, are not specifically courtly and are frequently used with little if any reference to the manners and preoccupations of life at Court. This is not so where courtly love is involved. As its name implies, the conventions which govern courtly love rely for their significance and even for their intelligibility upon the peculiar relationships which radiated from Court. When the Court ceases to be the centre of social existence and no longer enjoys a monopoly of sophisticated living, its manners, as well as much else, spread outward into society at large. As this change takes place during the sixteenth century, courtly love is drained of its significance and eventually emerges as courtship—a term which nevertheless serves to remind us that later romantic mannerisms and rituals derive from what was once the exclusive practise of the Court. It is,

however, no more than a reminder and by the 1590's, when Richard
Barnfield is writing in *The Shepheards Content* (1594),

> He is a Courtier, for he courts his love,

his use of *courts* is as old-fashioned as Shakespeare's use of *satisfaction* in
The Merchant of Venice.

The use of what appears on first sight to be a courtly lover's complaint is common in *The Shepheardes Calendar* and a passage from the
first of these, in the January Aeglogue, will serve to make the relevant
points about Spenser's use of the device. The following lines indicate
the state of the disconsolate lover after he has been rejected by his cruel
lady:

> You naked trees, whose shady leaues are lost,
> Wherein the byrds were wont to build their bowre:
> And now are clothd with mosse and hoary frost,
> Instede of bloosmes, wherwith your buds did flowre:
> I see your teares, that from your boughes doe raine,
> Whose drops in drery ysicles remaine.
>
> All so my lustfull leafe is drye and sere,
> My timely buds with wayling all are wasted . . .

A second glance will show that this is a lament rather than a complaint;
the mood is forlorn and mournful (both words are used a little later in
the Aeglogue to describe the state of the lover here) but there is no
suggestion of complaint. Indeed, far from complaining at the lover's
plight, the passage accepts it as perfectly natural; the imagery implying
that it is as natural, if as uncomfortable, as the coming of winter. Such a
use of imagery may be compared with that of Wyatt in the following
stanza (the second stanza of his poem "Resound my voyse"):

> Oft ye Revers, to here my wofull sounde,
>   Have stopt your course and, plainly to expresse
> Many a tere by moystor of the grounde,
>   The erth hath wept to here my hevenes;
>   Which causeles to suffre without redresse
> The howgy okes have rored in the wynde:
>   Eche me thought complayning in their kynde.
>   (XXII)

The relevant distinctions between the two passages are not immediately
obvious: in both the poet is using the natural setting to express the
lover's case. But in Wyatt nature storms on hearing of the lady's

cruelty; the rivers flood, the oaks roar: in Spenser nature calmly shrugs off its summer garb and dresses itself in winter, becoming "clothed with moss and hoary frost, Instede of bloosmes", its tears stilled in "drery ysicles". Wyatt's use of nature is similar to that of Shakespeare; the lady's departure from kindness (i.e. naturalness) meets with protest not only from the lover but from the whole of nature: in other words, Wyatt's conceit expresses the same metaphysical belief in human naturalness as we find in Shakespeare. For Spenser, on the other hand, the plight of the rejected lover is as much a part of the order of things as the coming of winter. And the passive acceptance of the lover's 'complaint' which this implies affects the character of the poetry in fairly obvious ways. The movement of the verse, for instance—

> You naked trees, whose shady leaues are lost,
> Wherein the byrds were wont to build their bowre

—realises a calm uniformity of mood which is not consistent with the declared condition of the rejected lover. The complacency of Colin is the result of Spenser's handling of the 'complaint'.

The spirit in which Spenser uses the 'complaint' is essentially the same as that in which he harks back to Chaucer. The poetry is given the appearance of the older courtly poetry by the use of a device. With the emphasis thus placed upon appearances it is not surprising that Spenser's view of what is natural should express itself in terms of dress and be devoid of the profounder implications which nature has in Wyatt and in Shakespeare.

Spenser's conception of style is a common one in Elizabethan poetry. The commendable desire of the *nouveaux riches* to acquire some veneer of sophistication, polish as we still call it, promotes an appreciation of style as appearance and reduces appearance to a garment, a dress clothing reality as a robe does a man. It is a view which finds its rationale in Elizabethan Platonism and drives Lear to strip off his furred gowns in a desperately pitiful search for "the thing itself".[8] Perhaps its most important consequence is the emergence of a poetic language which is essentially decorative and which, to quote Puttenham once again, elevates itself above "the common course of ordinary speech and capacitie of the vulgar iudgement" and so removes itself from the language of practical affairs.* Puttenham's comparison of a

* There was a parallel development in painting. It is in terms similar to Puttenham's that Nicholas Hillyarde, the miniaturist, praised the art he practised. It is, he wrote in his *Treatise Concerning the Arte of Limning,*

a thing apart from all other painting or drawing, and tendeth not to comon mens vsse,

proper poetic language to the court fashions of his day calls to mind
Veblen's opinion that the principal attraction of fashionable clothes in
the late-nineteenth century lay in a similar rejection of practicality, in
that they mutilated their wearers and rendered them "permanently
and obviously unfit for work".[9] That this was also true of women's
fashions in the late-sixteenth century is suggested by William Harrison's
reference to "their farthingales, and diversely coloured nether stocks of
silk, jersey, and such like, whereby their bodies are rather deformed
than commended".[10]

Ben Jonson shows himself fully alive to the consequences of the
argument from fashion when he urges the cause of "right and naturall
language" in *Timber*:

> Right and naturall language seemes to have least of the wit in it;
> that which is writh'd and tortur'd is counted the more exquisite.
> Cloath of Bodkin, or Tissue, must be imbrodered; as if no face were
> faire that were not pouldred or painted? No beauty to be had but in
> wresting and writhing our owne tongue? Nothing is fashionable
> till it bee deform'd; and this is to write like a *Gentleman*.* All must
> bee as affected and preposterous as our Gallants cloathes, sweet bags,
> and night dressings; in which you would thinke our men lay in,
> like *Ladies*, it is so curious.[11]

But it is Swift, at the end of the seventeenth century, who unintention-
ally reveals the full metaphysical implications of Elizabethan poetic
style as preached by Puttenham and illustrated by Spenser:

> Look on this globe of earth, you will find it to be a very complete
> and fashionable dress. What is that which some call land but a fine
> coat faced with green? or the sea, but a waist-coat of water-tabby?
> Proceed to the particular works of the creation, you will find how
> curious journeyman Nature has been to trim up the vegetable beaux;
> observe how sparkish a periwig adorns the head of a beach, and what
> a fine doublet of white satin is worn by the birch.
>   To conclude from all, what is man himself but a micro-coat, or
> rather a complete suit of clothes, with all its trimmings.[12]

either for furnishing of howsses or any patternes for tapistries, or building, or any other
work whatsoeuer, and yet it excelleth all other painting whatsoeuer in sondry points, in
giuing the true lustur to pearle and precious stone, and worketh the metals gold or
siluer with themselyes . . . benning fittest for the decking of princes bookes or to put in
jeuuels of gould and for the imitation of the purest flowers and most beautiful creaturs
in the finest coullers. . . Carl Winter, *Elizabethan Miniatures*, (London, 1955), p. 6.

* Jonson's jibe at the social pretensions of such a style is not gratuitous. Puttenham makes
it explicit that he advocates a style which will give the upstart some appearance of gentility.

In conjunction with the language of riches, the stylistic idioms of Elizabethan poetry, with their insistence upon appearance and decoration—what Sir John Davies in *Orchestra* (1594) called a "rhetoric clothing speech in rich array"—serve to define decorum in terms of conspicuous wealth. It is such a decorum we find exemplified in "Queene *Vertue*'s court" and, to take another example, in the opening stanza of Spenser's *Prothalamion*:

> Along the shoare of siluer streaming *Themmes*,
> Whose rutty Bancke, the which his Riuer hemmes,
> Was paynted all with variable flowers,
> And all the meades adornd with daintie gemmes,
> Fit to decke maydens bowres.

Here the awareness of scenic beauty is promoted by the equation between aesthetic attraction and costly artifice; nature is seen, if not quite as "a very complete and fashionable dress", certainly as an expensive piece of decoration, as painted flowers and gem-encrusted fields, the work of Puttenham's excellent painter and embroiderer adorning the stuff of a princely garment with precious stones.*

In the *Amoretti* (Sonnet LXX) spring appears as a product of the same couturiers:

> Fresh spring the herald of loues might king,
> In whose cote armour richly are displayd
> All sorts of flowers the which on earth do spring
> In goodly colours gloriously arrayd.

In isolation these lines might almost be considered one of Spenser's Chaucerisms, which, in Jonson's opinion, "were better expung'd and banish'd".[13] They have their parallel in the description of the young squire in the General Prologue to *The Canterbury Tales*:

> Embrouded was he, as it were a meede
> Al ful of fresshe floures, whyte and reede.

But Chaucer does not see nature as an artificiality—the 'meede' and the 'floures' are only illustrations—whereas Spenser does, his vision having been profoundly affected by the mystique of conspicuous wealth. It is not fortuitous that "richly are displayed" and "gloriously arrayed" are

---

* In much the same way Hillyarde's miniatures "combine the arts of the jeweller, goldsmith and medallist as accessories to the art of the painter" (Winter, pp. 12-13). His "jeweller's dream of capturing in paint the colours of diamond, sapphire, ruby, emerald, topaz and amethyst, his goldsmith's passion for decoration" provides the imaginative link with the Elizabethan poets which is remarked by Carl Winter (Winter, p. 8).

the two phrases that dominate Spenser's description of spring; they are the expressions of one who looks on "this globe of earth" as a "complete and fashionable dress".

This conception of style, expounded by Puttenham and embodied in the poetry of Sidney and Spenser, is deeply ingrained in the idioms of Elizabethan poetry, idioms which encourage those who, in Jonson's words, "labour onely to ostentation and are ever more busie about the colours and surface of a worke then in the matter and foundation".[14] Spenser's *Epithalamion* is referred to by the poet as a

> Song made in lieu of many ornaments,
> With which my loue should duly haue bene dect.

Daniel's country maid is "deckt with truth" and he thinks of women as "deckt with beauty". For Shakespeare, the sonneteer, truth is a "sweet ornament" that makes beauty more beautiful, whilst for another of his contemporaries beauty itself is only "a painted flower"[15]. The moon is "the silver ornament of night" and the spirit of night is attired, spangled, embroidered—

> Attired in black, spangled with flames of fire,
> Embroidered with stars in silent night.[16]

In Spenser's *Epithalamion* the lady's locks "do lyke a golden mantle her attyre" and, as has already been remarked, the meads of *Prothalamion* are "adorned with dainty gemmes". The Queen herself is for Sir John Davies the "best jewel that earth doth wear".[17] Nature too, in Elizabethan poetry, usually follows the advice of Puttenham: "the earth wears all her riches" and the skies are "enamelled with both the Indies' gold".[18] May, for instance, is a month "when skies blue silk, and meadows carpets be", "when Flora gilds the earth with golden flowers", and when the industrious bee,

> Enveloped in her sweet perfumed array,
> Doth leave his honey-lined delicious bowers,
> More richly wrought than prince's stately towers.[19]

Such imagery is not in itself new; Petrarch, for instance, refers to Laura as adorned with gold, pearls, and purple, in a phrase which may describe her features rather than her dress.[20] It is the widespread and persistent use of such imagery, with its continual insistence upon richness—"richly wrought", "richly are displayed"—which establishes Elizabethan poetic decorum as the expression of a life-style governed by the mystique of conspicuous wealth.

The selection of quotations given above could well have provided the text for Sidney's remark that "Nature never set forth the earth in so rich tapestry as divers poets have done". But it appears that in making this remark Sidney had some doubts as to the value of such a richly decorative view of poetry. These doubts emerge as we read the passage from which that remark has been taken:

Nature never set forth the earth in so rich tapestry as divers poets have done—neither with pleasant rivers, fruitful trees, sweet-smelling flowers, nor whatsoever else may make the too much loved earth more lovely. Her world is brazen, the poets only deliver a golden.[21]

In Puttenham, Spenser, Sidney, and their contemporaries, rich tapestry (synonymous with costly artifice and expensive decoration) is used to make "earth more lovely". It is of interest to note, therefore, that in this particular passage from the *Apology for Poetry* Sidney is critical of "rich tapestry"; it is true that it makes "earth more lovely", but the earth upon which the poets exercise their cosmetic craft is already "too much loved". Similarly, whilst nature's "world is brazen, the poets only deliver a golden". Sidney could have written "only the poets deliver a golden" had that been what was clearly meant; as it is the syntax betrays a barely suppressed awareness of the inadequacy of the golden world. What Sidney appears to half-realise is that the view of nature current in poetry is false, in that it misrepresents actuality and in that it misvalues it. Swift fully realises both the falsity and the ludicrousness of the view in his ironic exposition of it in *A Tale of A Tub*. Sidney, however, also comes close to recognising that this view is an expression of current poetic practise; that it is the poetic impulse which expresses itself in rich decoration and that the nature which is distorted in its rich and golden expression is the nature of poetry itself.

The awareness of the inadequacy of the golden world grows stronger and more articulate in the 1590's, encouraged by the changing character of Elizabethan social life. As the bourgeoisie develops as a distinct and independent class it creates, from the realities of its own economic existence, a life-style which finds expression and justification in Puritanism and particularly in the teachings of Calvin.

Such teaching, whatever its theological merits or defects, was admirably designed to liberate economic energies and to weld into a disciplined social force the rising *bourgeoisie*, conscious of the contrast between its own standards and those of a laxer world, proud of its vocation as the standard-bearer of the economic virtues, and determined to vindicate an open road for its own way of life by the use of every weapon . . .[22]

Simplicity and abstinence in both public and private life were preached by Puritanism and more forcefully enjoined by the doctrine of primitive capital accumulation, or thrift, the doctrine that

> The less you eat, drink and read books; the less you go to the theatre, the dance hall, the public-house; the less you think, love, theorize, sing, paint, fence, etc., the more you save—the greater becomes your treasure which neither moths nor rust will devour—your capital.[23]

The thrifty citizen looked upon the fine gowns of Puttenham's "Madames of honour" not only as pieces of conspicuous waste but as evidence of sin; as Thomas Whythorne observed of such fine ladies, "to manyfest and diskover their prowd harts, and lecherous lusts, thei do dek and attier them selves so flawnting and gloriowsly lyk peakoks".[24] This was to become the attitude of the self-respecting bourgeois, critical of his 'betters' rather than aping them and contemptuous of the advice which Puttenham offers the poetical upstart:

> that being now lately become a Courtier he shew not himself a craftsman, and merit to be disgraded, and with scorne sent back againe to the shop, or other place of his facultie and calling.[25]

Towards the end of the sixteenth century this new critical attitude creates a problem of style which finds a self-conscious reflection in Shakespeare's sonnets, in such questions and declarations as "Oh how thy worth with manners may I sing?" "My tongue-tied Muse in manners holds her still", "So all my best is dressing old words new". Amongst other things Shakespeare is remarking that although the particular worth with which he is concerned cannot find expression in conventional, mannered terms, he is reduced to Puttenham's couturier-like rôle of "dressing old words new". This distinction between manner and matter, between intrinsic worth and outward appearance or show, between artifice (often referred to by Shakespeare as art) and nature, poses in the Sonnets problems far wider than that of "how thy worth with manners may I sing?" Indeed this Shakespearian preoccupation with the problems of his art arises from the idioms of Elizabethan life rather than from the peculiar difficulties of poetry.

As in writing about his poetry Shakespeare distinguishes between manner and matter, so in general he distinguishes in the Sonnets between appearances (likened after the idiom of the time to raiment, painting and ornament) and inward worth. He writes of youth as "the world's fresh ornament" dressed in "youth's proud livery", refers to the Muse that is "Stirr'd by a painted beauty" and remarks that "that beauty that doth cover thee, is but the seemly raiment of my heart", that his guiding star "puts apparel on my tottered loving, To show me worthy of thy sweet respect", mentions "the ornament of beauty", and so on. In the latter half of the sonnet sequence Shakespeare's attitude towards outward show changes: he observes of cankered roses that "their virtue only is their show", that true beauty is "Without all ornament", that "outward form" can mislead one into believing a lively love is dead, that "dwellers on form" are likely to "Lose all"; he refers to "Art's false borrow'd face", to "Love's best habit" (i.e. dress) being "seeming trust", and finally asks, "Why dost thou pine within and suffer dearth Painting thy outward walls so costly gay?" before tendering the advice "Within be fed, without be rich no more".

Here, then, are two conflicting attitudes towards manner and outward appearance; the one sees in it an occasion for praise and respect, the other presents it with suspicion and distrust as the ground of falsehood, hypocrisy and spiritual impoverishment. The attitude which eventually prevails in the Sonnets is the second one, grounded in the perception that the measure of true worth is 'Within'. It is not sufficient that, in the words of sonnet 53, "In all external grace you have some part", for

> How like Eve's apple doth thy beauty grow,
> If they sweet virtue answer not thy show.

What Sonnet 16 calls "inward worth" must match the "outward fair". It is the abuse of such a union of appearance and intrinsic worth that is the concern of Sonnet 95:

> Oh what a mansion have those vices got,
> Which for their habitation chose out thee,
> Where beauty's veil doth cover every blot,
> And all things turns to fair, that eyes can see!

Forms, appearances and manners are not to be trusted; the concern is for something intrinsically human, not for apparel, painting, ornament, but for something "Richer than wealth, prouder than garment's cost". And plainness comes to appear as a positive virtue to Shakespeare, as it does to the Puritans:

> They rightly do inherit heaven's graces,
> And husband nature's riches from expense.

This conclusion reflects back upon Shakespeare's characterisation of his own poetry, as when in Sonnet 82 he refers to his language as "true plain words" and in Sonnet 83 declares,

> I never saw that you did painting need,
> And therefore to your fair no painting set.

It is a conclusion summed-up in the conviction of Sonnet 101 that "Truth needs no colour". Shakespeare's final view of the style of conspicuous wealth, then, agrees with Sidney's description of it as "that honey-flowing matron Eloquence apparelled, or rather disguised, in a courtesan-like painted affectation". His objection to it is that voiced by Thomas Whythorne:

> to flatter, glos, or ly . . . requyreth gloriowz and painted speech whereaz the trewth needeth but A plain and simpull vtterans with-owt glozing of faining at all.[26]

It was not an uncommon objection, especially amongst Puritans: Valentine Marshall professed "Nakedness . . . the best garnishing and Ornament the truth can have" and Richard Sibbes that when truth "is most naked, it is most lovely and powerful".[27]

In matters of dress and ornament more was involved for the Elizabethans than questions of taste and fashion. The conception of style defined by George Puttenham and informing much Elizabethan poetry cannot be abstracted from the fundamental movements shaping Elizabethan life. The dissolution of the monasteries and the looting of Church property redistributed not only Church lands but also such Church treasures as candlesticks, drinking vessels, rich embroideries and tapestries. It had an effect, that is to say, not only upon the economy but upon taste and fashion. For the goldsmiths, silversmiths, jewellers and embroiderers, whose principal market had long been the Church, this was a matter of some importance, since having been deprived of that market they had to direct their attention to the secular one. So that sequestration of Church property not only helped to create a body of *nouveaux riches*, it also released the craftsmen to form and gratify its taste and thereby produced numerous examples of the peacocks castigated by Whythorne, those "English peacocks" whom Nashe described as "painting themselves with church spoils".[28]

The controversy which prompted Whythorne's remark is that which broke out in the 1560's on the extravagance of female attire, but it has its more serious counterpart in the conflict of opinion on Church ornaments and vestments. This latter controversy was serious not because learned doctors disagreed but because of what was happening in the country, in Grantham for instance, where, in 1566,

> The Rood Mary, and John, and all other idols and pictures, mass-books, legend-books, and all other papistical books and ceremonies were openly burned at the cross called the Market Cross. . . . The vestments, copes, albs, tunicles, and all other such baggages were defaced and openly sold by a general consent of the whole corporation . . .[29]

Thus, whilst Puttenham's Court ladies flaunted themselves like peacocks, the citizens of Grantham were "painting themselves with church spoils" and raising issues which went far beyond taste and fashion.

From the point of view of taste and fashion, Protestantism was transforming the altar cloth into a doublet, the cope into a gown, the chalice into a drinking cup and the censer into a salt cellar. But it failed to capitalise the treasure 'liberated' from the Church and only succeeded in replacing ecclesiastical ostentation by the ostentation of the *nouveaux riches*. The Elizabethan love poets contributed to the task of secularisation; the images of the Blessed Virgin driven from the churches reappear as the ladies of Elizabethan love poetry,* their original iconography still apparent, however, in the gold, silver and jewels of their features.

The fundamental economic and aesthetic reformation did not get under way until the emergence of Puritanism in the 1580's. The Puritan was a capitalist, a man for whom the one true use of wealth was investment and to whom ostentation was a conspicuous waste of economic substance. All that did not conduce to thrift and devotion to work he looked upon as sinful vanity and pride: to encourage investment one must curtail consumer spending—that is the first axiom of Puritan aesthetics. In short, the Protestant Reformation turned wealth into merchandize; the Puritan Reformation turned it into capital. The difference in life-style which flows from this economic distinction was quite evident: on the one hand there were the resplendent garments of

---

* Should this seem a trifle far-fetched it needs to be pointed out that the Elizabethan Church's Book of Homilies anticipated Sidney's idolatory when (in the sermon mentioned in n. 24 to the present chapter) it criticised shipmen for singing, *Ave, maria Stella* to our Lady. In the same place (*op. cit.*, p. 236) it asks,

> when you hear of our lady of Walsingham, our lady of Ipswich, our lady of Wilsdon, and such other; what is it but an imitation of the Gentiles idolaters? Diana Agrotera, Diana Coryphea, Diana Ephesia, Venus Cypria, Venus Paphia, Venus Gnidia.

D

Puttenham's "Madames of honour", on the other the "plaine and simple apparell" of the Puritan matron. It is the emergence of the new, Puritan ideology which leads to the decline of the rich and ornate style that dominates Elizabethan poetry and to its replacement by the plainer style of the early seventeenth century.

3. THE COMMERCE OF AFFECTION

In the common metaphors which it employs to figure forth the love relationship, Elizabethan poetry provides ample evidence of the chains and fetters which limit the range of its sensibility and of the forms of association which forged them. Michael Drayton's sonnet "To such as say thy love I overprize", for instance, is a late sixteenth century counterpart of Wyatt's sonnet "The longe love". As Wyatt's sonnet places love within the social nexus of a still feudal England, so Drayton's sonnet offers a definition of love in terms of a capitalist society; in the earlier poem the lover is a squire serving his lord, in the later poem he is a speculator playing the market. Replying "To such as say thy love I over-prize", Drayton defines his love in the explanation that

> Though I give more than well affords my state,
> In which expense the most suppose me vain,
> Which yields them nothing at the easiest rate,
> Yet at this price returns me treble gain.
> They value not, unskilful how to use,*
> And I give much, because I gain thereby:
> I that thus take, or they that thus refuse,
> Whether are these deceived then, or I?[1]

The ease with which love enters the money-market here, and with which that market confers its own evaluations upon love, is suggestive of the forces which are at work establishing wealth as something intrinsically honourable.

In a world which had awakened from the dream of alchemy to find it had the Midas touch, it is hardly surprising that attitudes to people and the relationships between them begin to assume a pecuniary character. The poetry of the time faithfully reflects this. The products and activities of the Mint, for instance, had become distinctly poetical by the end of the sixteenth century, much as birds and their songs did at the beginning of the nineteenth. The commonest of all human activities, speech, is a kind of money-making to Dowland when he writes that his tongue

* Here *to use* means "to practise usury".

> makes my mouth a mint
> And stamps my thoughts to coin them words by art.[2]

Rankins uses the same metaphor in writing of the man whose "copper words come out of coxecombs mint"[3]; an idiom which has become so entrenched that nowadays few people realise they are using one when they speak of coining phrases. Shakespeare represents political authority in similar terms when Angelo appeals to the Duke in *Measure for Measure* (I.1.48–50):

> Let there be some more test made of my metal,
> Before so noble and so great a figure
> Be stamped upon it.

And Donne is most adept at coining and minting insignia for his love (in "A Valediction: of weeping", for instance) and in "The Canonisation" advises his reader to

> Observe his honour, or his grace,
> Or the King's real, or his stamped face
> Contemplate.

Rankins had already made his choice between the real and the stamped face when he praised Cynthia, the Queen, "whose soueraigne beauty coynes doth disclaime".[4] But it is perhaps Davies of Hereford who waxes most lyrical over the mint condition of Cynthia, who, he confesses,

> Mak'st me still sleep in love, whose golden dreams
> Give love right current—sith well-coined-delight.[5]

There is a certain logic in imagining love as money, for it is the means by which the lover purchases his lady. In "Lovers' Infiniteness" Donne declares that he has exhausted the conventional gestures of a lover in lines which stress the expensiveness of love:

> And all my treasure, which should purchase thee—
> Sighs, tears, and oaths, and letters—I have spent;
> Yet no more can be due to me,
> Than at the bargain made was meant.

Love here is realised in the market-place; the lover is a would-be purchaser whose lack of thrift prevents him from paying the agreed price for the lady. In the remainder of the poem the conceit develops

into a legal quibble concerning the pre-emptive right of a land purchaser to the future products of his purchase.*

Sidney also describes the love relationship as a commercial transaction, in which

> My true love hath my hart, and I have his,
> By just exchange, one for the other giv'ne.
> I holde his deare, and myne he cannot misse:
> There never was a better bargaine driv'ne.[6]

Chapman, meriting his name with his description of night as "love's
mart of kisses", and the author of the anonymous song "Silly Boy,
there is no cause", in his reference to "They that go to Cupid's mart",[7]
express the same bazaar appreciation of love as Donne and Sidney. And
if in the case of "Queen *Vertue's* court" one is tempted, as a way of
putting an objection, to say that Sidney writes of Stella in the spirit
of an enthusiastic salesman, this comes closer to literal truth in one
of Spenser's amoretti:

> Ye tradefull Merchants, that with weary toyle,
> do seeke most pretious things to make your gain;

* Rankins also plays with the complications of real estate in a metaphor which, according to his editor, chides "mighty men" who pretend to be the authors of books they have
employed other men to write for them:

> When mighty men must haue their wisdome lent,
> And being landlordes buy their wit for rent.
> In fine, the fyne he payes will come to light,
> And all be forfait to the foole by right.
>   (*Op cit.*, satyr quartos, lines 11–14)

The editor's interpretation of this conceit is probably wrong simply because he has not
appreciated that the allusion is to a saying which changed its sense with the rise of
commerce. The saying appears in Heywood's *Proverbs* (1546) as *wit is never good till it
be bought* and there is a variant of it in *Tottel's Miscellany* (1557), in the poem, "The
wise trade of lyfe":

> Do all you dedes by good aduise,
> Cast in your minde alwaies the end.
> Wit bought is of to dere a price . . .

Here *bought* plainly means "acquired by experience". However, as, with the rise of
commerce, the dominant sense of *bought* becomes "purchased for money", the saying
wit is never good till it be bought comes to mean that it is better to purchase the wit of others
than to cultivate one's own and we are told in *Conceits, Clinches, Flashes and Whimzies*
(1639) that 'Stationers could not live, if men did not beleeve the old saying, that Wit
bought is better than Wit taught." It is to this later opinion that Rankins objects. He does
not object to men pretending to be the authors of books they have paid other men to write,
but to men relying for their wisdom upon books rather than upon direct experience and
knowledge of the world. His attitude is similar to that later adopted by Bacon, Hobbes,
and Descartes, who opposed personal knowledge to the authority of scholastic texts.
He returns to the conceit of land mortgage in *satyrus peregrinans* (lines 116–19).

and both the Indias of their treasures spoile,
  what needeth you to seeke so farre in vaine?
For loe my loue doth in her selfe containe
  all this worlds riches that may farre be found,
  if Saphyres, loe her eies be Saphyres plaine,
  if Rubies, loe hir lips be Rubies sound:
If Pearles, hir teeth be pearles both pure and round;
  if Yuorie, her forhead yuory weene;
  if siluer, her faire hands are siluer sheene.
But that which fairest is, but few behold,
  her mind adornd with vertues manifold.

Spenser is paraphrasing a sonnet by Philipe Desportes, "Marchans qui traversez tout rivage More", but he was not alone in finding this French poem particularly attractive; there is another paraphrase of it in *Emaricduse* (1595), a volume of sonnets by 'E.C.' Browne's "Song of the Sirens" from *The Inner Temple Masque* (1615) contains similar advice to those who sail in search of riches.* There is nothing particularly subtle or obscure about the scheme of significant relations in Spenser's sonnet, a scheme linking 'this worlds riches', 'fairest' and 'adornd', that is to say, wealth, beauty and ornamentation. This formula defines the sense in which Spenser's sonnet observes an Elizabethan decorum. As a complimentary poem it flatters the lady by treating her as a precious but as yet unexploited commodity. An anonymous contemporary of Spenser addresses "tradefull Merchants" in a similar vein:

What needeth all this travail and turmoiling,
  Shortening the life's sweet pleasure
  To seek this far-fetched treasure
  In those hot climates under Phoebus broiling?

* Browne's "Song of the Sirens" begins,

Steer hither, steer your winged pines,
  all beaten mariners!
Here lie love's undiscovered mines,
  A prey to passengers;
Perfumes far sweeter than the best
Which make the Phoenix' urn and nest.
  Fear not your ships,
Nor any to oppose you save our lips;
  But come on shore
Where no joy dies till love hath gotten more.

In Shakespeare's *The Merchant of Venice* Salerio recounts the merchants' fears to which the Sirens refer and Bassanio chooses the easier way to fortune which they hold out to "beaten mariners" (see pp. 54–5 below).

> O fools, can you not see a traffic nearer
> In my sweet lady's face, where Nature showeth
> Whatever treasure eye sees or heart knoweth?
> Rubies and diamonds dainty,
> And orient pearls such plenty,
> Coral and ambergris sweeter and dearer
> Than which the South Seas or Moluccas lend us,
> Or either Indies, East or West, do send us.[8]

Donne also sees the "traffic nearer" and describes his mistress enthusiastically as "My America! my new-found-land...! My mine of pretious stones" in *Elegy XIX*.

   Love in Elizabethan poetry is (as Thersites says of Ajax) "bought and sold among those of any wit, like a barbarian slave".[9] In Shakespeare's *The Merchant of Venice* Bassanio and Portia's other suitors are seen as merchants doing precisely what Spenser and his anonymous contemporary would have them do.* When Bassanio explains to Antonio his project for recouping his losses and making his fortune by winning Portia, that she is fair and virtuous are added attractions; he thinks of her first as a rich heiress. Consequently his use of such terms as 'undervalued', 'worth', 'golden fleece', 'thrift', and 'fortunate', is disturbingly economic:

> In Belmont is a lady richly left,
> And she is fair, and, fairer than that word,
> Of wondrous virtues. . . .
> Her name is Portia, nothing undervalued
> To Cato's daughter, Brutus' Portia—
> Nor is the wide world ignorant of her worth,
> For the four winds blow in from every coast

---

* It should be noted that Shakespeare's most famous lovers, Romeo and Juliet, use the commercial idiom to express their love. Thus Romeo declares to Juliet,

> I am not pilot; yet wert thou as far
> As that vast shore washed with the furthest sea,
> I would adventure for such merchandise. (II.ii.82–4)

Here Romeo imagines himself to be a merchant adventurer willing to take a great risk for the sake of a rich reward. It is, I believe, significant that the phrase "a rich reward" cannot adequately convey the pecuniary sense I wish to bring to the attention, because this sense is so intricately connected in our culture, and so in our imaginations, with fullness of life; *rich* means this too and merchandising here can be relied upon to suggest the enhancement ('enrichment') of life. The fact that we can move so easily and often so unwittingly from the now primary sense of *rich* (possessed of material wealth) to the subsidiary senses (e.g. Shakespeare's "widowed wombs rich with big increase") is an illustration of the manner in which a bourgeois ideology has affected our mental and imaginative processes.

Renowned suitors, and her sunny locks
Hang on her temples like a golden fleece,
Which makes her seat of Belmont Colchos' strand,
And many Jasons come in quest of her . . .
O my Antonio, had I but the means
To hold a rival place with one of them,
I have a mind pressages me such thrift,
That I should questionless be fortunate.

(I.i.161–77)

The reference to Jason is peculiarly apt, for Bassanio is one of a company of Elizabethan lovers who see themselves as new Argonauts adventuring to bring home a golden fleece. Drummond thinks of his lady's hair, as we have already seen (p. 33 above), as richer than the product of Colchian mines, and Rankins alludes to Colchis as a land of amorous disport where the sun always shines:

> The sun shines where the golden Fleece doth rest,
> Where Ladyes wanton with a carpet band,
> (Though it be shut) within the Misers chest.

The relevance of these lines to an understanding of Bassanio's position may be judged from the editor's note:

> 'Band' certainly alludes to the bond which the usurer has safely locked up in his chest, but it may also pun on 'bond', a base fellow. 'Carpet' is apparently in the usual sense of inactive, boudoir-haunting. Perhaps we should interpret: where ladies flirt with a base fellow who lives in society only because he has mortgaged his property to a usurer for ready money, and so can shine as a gentleman for a time.[10]

Bassanio has gambled away his property in previous adventures and it is his friend, Antonio, who enters into a bond with the usurious Shylock so that Bassanio "can shine as a gentleman" long enough to win a rich heiress and so repair his fortunes. Bassanio is a merchant adventurer in whose imagination Portia is "a stately merchant ship which brings to her husband riches and credit".* Following the advice of the poets to

---

* See p. 34 above, and note. *Credit* is a richly meaningful word here. Like so many words, its dominant sense changes with the rise of commerce. It means 'honour', of course, but it also has that fiscal sense in which it is used by Antonio and which is probably its primary one in current usage. It marks that convergence of honour and financial stability which was remarked by Whythorne—"akkording to the quantite of a mans substans thei akkownt him honest, and so to bee kredited and beleeved" (see p. 24 above)—and is one of the new idioms against which he protests.

"tradefull Merchants" he pursues the "traffic nearer", whilst his more conventional friends are

> Plucking the grass to know where sits the wind;
> Peering in maps for ports, and piers, and roads.
>
> (I.i.18–19)

This kind of fortune-hunting was often remarked. Rankins tells a story of "certaine sharkers" who disguised a boy player as a girl and introduced him to a gallant.

> They soone perswaded him she was an heyre,
> And onely daughter to a knight well knowne,
> He saw her young, rich, amorous and faire,
> Haue her he must, or dye he would with moane,
> In sleepy nights his very soule did groane.[11]

And Burton records that

> Many men if they do hear but of a good portion, a rich heir, are more mad than if they had all the beauteous ornaments, and those good parts art and nature can afford, they care not for honesty, bringing up, birth, beauty, person, but for money. . . . If she be rich, then she is fair, fine, absolute and perfect, then they burn like fire, they love her dearly . . .[12]

Rankins and Burton not only define for us the bourgeois impulse to courtship, and so enhance our awareness of the nature of Bassanio's romantic inclinations, they also demonstrate the manner in which the old courtly-love conceits, of the unrequited lover who burns like fire and tosses and turns through sleepless nights, are given a thoroughly bourgeois application.

There is something to be said in favour of Bassanio's way of getting rich. He could argue, with Volpone and Mosca,

> I wound no earth with ploughshares, fat no beasts
> To feed the shambles; have no mills for iron,
> Oil, corn, or men, to grind them into powder:
> I blow no subtle grass, expose no ships
> To threat'nings of the furrow-faced sea;
> I turn no monies in the public bank,
> No usurer private.

He does not

Tear forth the fathers of poor families
Out of their beds, and coffin them alive
In some kind clasping prison, where their bones
May be forthcoming, when the flesh is rotten. [13]

His method of acquiring wealth may seem more civilised than Salerio's
or Shylock's, but in actuality it is to raise money from a usurer (by
placing his friend at risk) and with it to finance a merchant's venture
which proves 'fortunate'. The whole process provides a striking
illustration of bourgeois courtship and friendship and, since we still live
in a dominantly bourgeois society, it is understandable that C. L.
Barber should look upon the process as a demonstration of "the beni-
ficence of civilized wealth". [14] The oddness of that judgment only makes
itself felt when one begins to question the equation between civilisation and business. The civilisation to which C. L. Barber alludes is that
of Shylock's daughter, Jessica, as she gilds herself with ducats in order
to make herself more attractive in the eyes of Lorenzo (II.vi.49–50).★
We may well see Jessica in this scene not only as the embodiment of
More's Lady Money and the Lady Pecunia of Barnfield and Jonson, [15]
but also as the highest expression of the gilded lady of Elizabethan love
poetry.

There is little suggestion that Shakespeare is critical of the commercialisation of love. Although Gratiano's response to Jessica's
decision to gild herself with ducats, "Now, by my hood, a Gentile,
and no Jew" (II.vi.51) glances ironically at the behaviour of the Vene-
tian merchants, the general tendency of the play is to support spending
and risking, i.e. 'honest' mercantilism, against hoarding and usury.†

★ It is the civilisation of Sir John Harington's "Fair, rich, and young" (*Epigrams*, 1618)
—"Fair, rich, and young: how rare is her perfection". Its characteristic utterances are those
of Ayton's "On a Woman's Inconstancy"—

> God send me love, my debts to pay,
> While unthrifts fool their love away!

—and Beaumont's "True Beauty"—

> May I find a woman rich,
> And not of too high a pitch:
> If that pride should cause disdain,
> Tell me lover, where's thy gain?

The ducats perform the same service for Jessica as the lady's locks, which "Do lyke a
golden mantle her attyre", perform for the lady in Spenser's *Epithalamion*.

† The practise of hoarding was generally frowned upon. That men should not cultivate
a cloistered virtue but put it to some public use is also the substance of the Duke's homily
in *Measure for Measure*, I.i.29–35. By the same principle, distribution was held to be the

Until the end of the sixteenth century he appears content with the commercial idioms of Elizabethan love poetry. In the *Sonnets*, for instance, it is not uncommon to discover a naïve economism skilfully regulating the logic of the affections, as in Sonnet 4:

> Unthrifty loveliness why dost thou spend
> Upon thyself thy beauty's legacy?
> Nature's bequest gives nothing but doth lend,
> And being frank she lends to those are free:
> Then beauteous niggard why dost thou abuse
> The bounteous largess given thee to give?
> Profitless usurer why dost thou use
> So great a sum of sums yet canst not live?
> For having traffic with thyself alone,
> Thou of thyself thy sweet self dost deceive,
> Then how when nature calls thee to be gone,
> What acceptable audit canst thou leave?
> > Thy unus'd beauty must be tomb'd with thee,
> > Which used lives th'executor to be.

The youth is criticised for indulging in an irregular form of commerce, "For having traffic with thyself alone", in a conceit which skilfully transfers to the youth's narcissism a disapproval otherwise reserved for the profitless usurer. The skill is there in the ease with which the equation between self-love and unprofitable money-lending is established, in the facility with which the affections are subjected to economic criteria.*

prime obligation laid upon the rich man by his riches. Men are wrong, argues the *Book of Homilies*, in supposing

> that by hoarding and laying up still, they shall at length be rich, and that by distributing and laying out, although it be for most necessary and godly uses, they shall be brought to poverty. (*Certain Sermons and Homilies*, p. 420.)

This is the opinion to which the following sonnet (Sonnet 4) subscribes.

* For the antithesis of Shakespeare's sonnet see Sonnet 10 of Drayton's *Idea*:

> To nothing fitter can I thee compare
> Than to the son of some rich penny-father,
> Who having now brought on his end with care,
> Leaves to his son all he had heaped together;
> This new rich novice, lavish of his chest,
> To one man gives, doth on another spend,
> Then here he riots, yet amongst the rest
> Haps to lend some to one true honest friend.
> Thy gifts thou in obscurity doth waste,
> False friends thy kindness, born to deceive thee;

At a guess I would judge that about a third of Shakespeare's 154 sonnets employ conceits of a similar nature. It might be objected that in Sonnet 4 the use of the conceit gives added weight to the poet's disapproval of the youth's behaviour. But the submission of the affections to economic criteria is not peculiar to sonnets which reprimand and disapprove. In Sonnet 30, for example, a similar conceit is used to establish the reality of the lover's grief:

> Then can I grieve at grievances foregone,
> And heavily from woe to woe tell o'er
> The sad account of fore-bemoaned moan,
> Which I new pay, as if not paid before.
>   But if the while I think on thee (dear friend)
>   All losses are restor'd, and sorrows end.

The same metaphor, of the lover set down before his account book, is more extensively relied upon by Michael Drayton in the third sonnet of his *Idea*:

> Taking my pen, with words to cast my woe,
> Duly to count the sum of all my cares,
> I find my griefs innumerable grow,
> The reckonings rise to millions of despairs;
> And thus, dividing of my fatal hours,
> The payments of my love I read and cross;
> Subtracting, set my sweets unto my sours,
> My joy's arrearage leads me to my loss:
> And thus, mine eyes a debtor to thine eye
> Which by extortion gaineth all their looks,
> My heart hath paid such grievous usury,
> That all their wealth lies in thy beauty's books:
> And all is thine which hath been due to me,
> And I a bankrupt, quite undone by thee.

Here, as in Shakespeare's sonnet, grief is treated in a spirit of cool, egotistical calculation. It is the presence of this same calculating spirit that defines the amorous stance of Sidney's "Queene *Vertue's* court" and

> Thy love, that is on the unworthy placed,
> Time hath thy beauty, which with age will leave thee;
>   Only that little which to me was lent
>   I give thee back when all the rest is spent.

The poem isn't an ancestor of Pope's lines upon old Cotta and his son in the *Epistle to Bathurst*, for unlike Pope's lines these form a conceit in which kindness, love and beauty (the young man's natural "gifts") are represented in terms of money. Drayton's Sonnet 58 in *Idea* is similar in conceit to Shakespeare's sonnet.

Spenser's "Ye tradefull Merchants" as thoroughly bourgeois and vulgar. Indeed, the conceit used by Shakespeare and Drayton can be traced back to Sidney's *Astrophil and Stella* (Sonnet 18):

> With what sharpe checkes I in my selfe am shent,
>   When into Reason's audite I do go:
>   And by just counts my selfe a banckrout know
> Of all those goods, which heav'n to me hath lent:
> Unable quite to pay even Nature's rent,
> Which unto it by birthright I do ow:
> And which is worse, no good excuse can show,
> But that my wealth I have most idly spent.

There is a detailed similarity between these lines and Shakespeare's Sonnet 4, but the general likeness between Sidney's sonnet, Drayton's sonnet "Taking my pen" and Shakespeare's Sonnet 30 is more significant: in all four the lover weighs up his profits and losses like a businessman preparing a balance sheet.

It would be naïve to call such conceits far-fetched; they are the natural expressions of minds so perfectly attuned to their social surroundings that their erotic enthrallment is most aptly defined by the convergence of account book and billet-doux. And so, where he requires a conceit to express the depth of a lover's grief, Shakespeare finds one in the image of a shopkeeper poring over his accounts and (a touch of bourgeois pathos) paying them twice over! This makes his friend a very "dear friend" indeed. However, the happy thought that the friend is 'worth' so much expense finally dispels the gloom, as, in much the same way, the fact that Portia is "richly left" buoys up Bassanio's hopes.

4. THE NEW RELIGION

The Elizabethans did not discover gold; it had long had its special uses and long been employed as a means of exchange. Chaucer humorously played off its exchange value against its use value in his epigram upon the Doctor of Physic:

> For gold in phisik is a cordial,
> Therefore he lovede gold in special.[1]

Gold had its mystique in Chaucer's day, when it was thought an instrument of the devil, but it had an entirely different one for the Elizabethans. Donne clearly indicates the source of its occult powers when he distinguishes between its natural properties and imagined virtues (it was thought the purest metal because it was refined rather than corrupted by fire)[2] and its social function in a usurious and mercantile economy:

> I, when I value gold, may think upon
> The ductileness, the application,
> The wholesomeness, the ingenuity,
> From rust, from soil, from fire ever free:
> But if I love it, 'tis because 'tis made
> By our new nature (Use) the soul of trade.[3]

John Wheeler, in his *Treatise of Commerce* (1601), remarks that Elizabethan life had become acutely mercenary, a matter of "one bargaine or another, chopping, changing, or some other kinde of contract".[4] And, as Donne observes, the consequent growth of usury (*Use*) produces in man a "new nature". Henceforth, avarice ceases to be looked upon as a vicious aberration and is accepted as a natural human impulse providing the one sure social dynamic: private greed becomes a public virtue and the moral foundation of capitalist society.

It is not surprising, therefore, to learn from Helen White that during the transitional period of the sixteenth century, when men were still unable to square their consciences to the new facts of social life, "of all the motives to sin in this region of man's relations to man, there is no question as to which the sixteenth century preacher put first. It was greed, the greed for wealth."[5]

"No man can be ignorant", Bacon wrote to King James, "of the idolatry that is generally committed in these degenerate times to money, as if it could do all things public and private."[6] The complaint was commonplace, even amongst those whose poetry elsewhere subscribes to the idolatry, such as Richard Barnfield:

> There are so many *Danaes* nowadays,
> That loue for lucre; paine for gaine is sold:
> No true affection can their fancie please,
> Except it be a *Ioue*, to raine downe gold,
> Into their laps, which they wyde open hold . . .[7]

Elizabethan love poetry is the hymnal of this idolatry, an idolatry which infuses the old compliments and appraisals with a new significance and produces its own *amour propre*. Although it obviously makes its effect felt upon Protestantism, it is not, as Weber urged, itself the spirit of Protestantism. One of the sermons appointed to be read in

Elizabethan churches makes it quite plain that the Protestant establishment believed that alterations in religion were being produced by the anti-religious forces of covetousness:

> ... the inclination of man to have his own holy devotions, devised new sects and religions ... with many holy and godly traditions and ordinances, (as it seemed by the outward appearance and goodly glistering of the works), but in very deed all tending to idolatry, superstition, and hypocrisy; their hearts within being full of ... covetousness.[8]

Nevertheless, whilst attacking the covetousness of the age, Protestantism is forced to come to terms with capitalism; the Puritans in particular, as William Haller has pointed out, "were endeavouring to adapt Christian morality to the needs of a population which was being steadily driven from its old feudal status into the untried conditions of competition between man and man in an increasingly commercial society under a money economy".[9] The adoration of wealth, however, is neither Protestant nor Roman Catholic, it is ecumenical. Wealth is a religion in its own right, capable of commanding allegiance within the citadels of the old faith, as Salerio enables us to see in the opening scene of *The Merchant of Venice* (I.i.29–36) when he enquires,

> Should I go to church
> And see the holy edifice of stone,
> And not bethink me straight of dangerous rocks,
> Which touching but my gentle vessel's side,
> Would scatter all her spices on the stream,
> Enrobe the roaring waters with my silks,
> And, in a word, but even now worth this,
> And now worth nothing.

Salerio's mercenary interests are represented by him as understandably turning his heart from God. He does not put the matter in quite that way, but the Elizabethans had been taught that

> Whosoever in time of reading God's word is careful in his mind of worldly business, of money, or of lucre, he is turned from God.[10]

For Salerio the "edifice of stone" is still 'holy', but the soul of his religion, that which captures and inspires his imagination, is wealth. Where once the church had put men in remembrance of immortality, in fear of their sins and in hope of their salvation, it now stands for Salerio as a reminder of the hazards of commercial enterprise; the gentle vessel he fears for is not his immortal soul but his richly laden merchantman.

The vision of heaven which one imagines a Salerio entertaining is similar to that which the Elizabethan lover had of his lady. In poems such as "Jerusalem, my happy home" (1601) conspicuous wealth is beatified:

> Thy walls are all of precious stones,
>   Thy streets paved with gold;
> Thy gates are eke of precious pearl
>   Most glorious to behold.
>
> Thy turrets and thy pinnacles
>   With diamonds do shine:
> Thy houses, covered are with gold,
>   Most perfect, pure, and fine.[11]

Much the same vision of heaven is provided by Raleigh in "The Passionate Man's Pilgrimage":

> Then the holy paths we'll travel,
> Strewed with rubies thick as gravel.
> Ceilings of diamonds, sapphire floors,
> High walls of coral, and pearl bowers.[12]

This view of heaven produces its own definition of the blessed, one which occurs in the self-congratulations of Donne—

> My Myne of precious stones, My Emperie,
> How blest am I in this discovering thee

—and of Shakespeare—

> So am I as the rich whose blessed key
> Can bring him to his sweet up-locked treasure.[13]

Rankins also sees heaven as a coffer to which the blessed have the key:

> Thou Treasurer of heauen where hast thou clos'd
> This hidden wealth of man's true happiness?
> In nothing humane fancy hath compos'd
> Yet on the earth once dwelt this blessedness,
> To bring the earth from cursed wretchedness:
> Open that secret coffer that we may see,
> (If not possess) that heauenly treasury.[14]

If "man's true happiness" may be considered "Nature's chiefest treasure", then Rankins' answer to Sidney's question, "Who keeps the key to Nature's chiefest treasure?" is that it is the Treasurer of Heaven, St. Peter. But the idiom which both Sidney and Rankins use turns the holy saint into a rich miser (as the same idiom "turns crowned kings to merchants" in Shakespeare's *Troilus and Cressida*). The transformation is characteristic of the changes effected by the new religion. The spirit at work here, as in Salerio's speech, is that which is busy in Elizabethan love poetry, shaping and resubstantiating religious experience as surely as it does love and friendship, beauty, virtue and honour.

The sentiments of Donne, Shakespeare and Rankins are also those of an anonymous poem written some thirty years earlier and, ironically, addressed to "My dear lady". In this poem, too, the lover congratulates himself upon his blessed state:

> Am not I in blessed case,
> Treasure and pleasure to possess?*

And it is this new dispensation, this new state of blessedness, which is elaborated upon by Jonson in the familiar opening lines of *Volpone*, in which Volpone is discovered at his matins:

> Good morning to the day; and next, my gold!
> Open the shrine, that I may see my saint . . .
>   let me kiss,
> With adoration, thee, and every relic
> Of sacred treasure in this blessed room. . . .
>   Dear Saint,
> Riches, the dumb god, that giv'st all men tongues,
> That can'st do nought, and yet mak'st men do all things;
> The price of souls; even hell, with thee to boot,
> Is made worth heaven. Thou art virtue, fame,
> Honour, and all things else. Who can get thee,
> He shall be noble, valiant, honest, wise . . .

What is offered here is a fuller characterisation of Shakespeare's "the rich whose blessed key Can bring him to his sweet up-locked treasure". Barnfield had already described Lady Pecunia as the goddess of the age and Burton was later to agree with him, declaring that "the goddess we adore is *Dea Moneta*, Queen Money, to whom we daily offer sacrifice".[15] That wealth was also the price of souls, as Volpone claims, was an opinion shared by John Wheeler, who, in his defence of commerce,

---

* Daniel supplies the answer to this question in *Rosamond* (1592) lines 785–6:

> Iudge those whom chance depriues of sweetest treasure,
> What tis to lose a thing we hold so deere. . . .

reminded his readers of those "subtill and cunning merchants . . . which haue made merchandise of men's soules".[16] The same conceit is used by Dekker to remind churchmen of their duty:

> Many Merchants hath this Cittie to her sonnes, of al which you are the most noble, you trafficke onely for mens soules, sending them to the Land of Promise, and the heauenly Ierusalem, and reciuing from thence (in Exchange) the richest Commoditie in the world, your owne saluation. O therefore bee not Slothfull: for if being chosen Pilots, you Sleepe, and so sticke vpon Rockes, you hazard your owne shipwracke more than theirs that venture with you.[17]

That wealth was virtue and honour, as Volpone further maintains, is borne out by the poetry of Sidney, Spenser, Donne and others; it is a truth of the age most succinctly expressed by a later writer who remarked that "you may arrive at riches, and riches in the end bring you to honour".[18]

The new religion finds its most familiar expression in the speech of Shakespeare's disillusioned Timon:[19]

> Gold! yellow, glittering, precious gold! No gods,
> I am no idle votarist. Roots, you clear heavens!
> Thus much of this will make black white, foul fair,
> Wrong right, base noble, old young, coward valiant.
> Ha! you gods, why this? What this, you gods? Why this
> Will lug your priests and servants from your sides,
> Pluck stout men's pillows from below their heads:
> This yellow slave
> Will knit and break religions; bless the accurs'd . . .*

As Marx remarked, writing of these lines, gold is presented as "the visible divinity—the transformation of all human and natural properties into their contraries, the universal confounding and overturning of things: it makes brothers of impossibilities".[20] Timon's "I am no idle votarist" is a truth, albeit a bitter one. He and Volpone expressly admit what is only an implication in the work of many Elizabethan poets;

---

* See also Dekker, *Old Fortunatus* (1599) I.i.303–10:

> My choice is store of gold; the rich are wise.
> He that upon his back rich garments wears,
> Is wise, though on his head grow Midas' ears.
> Gold is the strength, the sinews of the world,
> The health, the soul, the beauty most divine,
> A mask of gold hides all deformities;
> Gold is Heaven's physic, life's restorative,
> Oh therefore make me rich.

they acknowledge that wealth has possessed itself of the powers of a deity, that gold has become "the world's soul" and that

> Well did wise poets, by thy glorious name,
> Title that age which they would have the best;
> Thou being the best of things, and far transcending
> All style of joy, in children, parents, friends,
> Or any other waking dream on earth.[21]

Little wonder, then, that (in the words of Thomas Dekker) "the thrifty citizen . . . seeing the golden age returned into the world again, resolves to worship no saint but money".[22]

Plainly the appraisals made by the thrifty Elizabethan citizen, whether of love, beauty, virtue, honour or holiness, differ from those met with in the poetry of the earlier sixteenth century because they are part of the mystique of a different society. The values acknowledged in Wyatt's poetry belong to the feudal world of courtly love. As G. L. Brook has observed, an

> important characteristic of courtly love wherever it was found was that it was aristocratic. It grew up in a feudal society, and the love of a troubadour was thought of in terms of feudal relations. The lover devoted himself to the service of his mistress, who became his liege lady. He was her *baillie*, and had to render her the submission of a vassal.* The submission which a lover owed to his lady did not conflict with his feudal obligations as a knight; in fact, it was thought that a noble could not be a true knight unless he loved a lady, to please whom he performed his warlike deeds. Jeanroy points out that such a conception of the relations between a lady and her lover would be likely to grow up in a typical Provencal castle in which there were very few women of rank but many landless knights, squires, and pages, who were feudally inferior to the lady of the castle.
>
> This relationship helps to explain the extreme humility which is one of the characteristics of courtly love. Another result of the association between courtly love and feudalism was that knightly qualities, especially courtesy and loyalty, which would in any case be desirable in a lover, came to be especially valued.[23]

---

* *Vid.* E. K. Chambers, "Some Aspects of Medieval Lyric" in *Sir Thomas Wyatt and Some Collected Studies* (London, 1933), p. 50: "The love of the trouvére is conceived on the analogy of feudal relations. He vows himself to the service of a mistress, who becomes his liege lady. He is in her *baillie*, her *seignorie*. He must render her the submission of a vassal." Brook has mistaken the sense of *baillie*, which is not "one to whom goods are delivered, in bailment" (i.e. bailee) but "the outer wall of a feudal castle" (i.e. bailey).

In the Elizabethan age the appraisals we meet with do not emerge from the world of feudal obligation referred to by Brook, but from one in which, as John Wheeler, one-time Secretary of the Merchant Adventurers, observed in 1601,

> there is nothing . . . so ordinarie, and naturall vnto men, as to contract, truck, merchandise, and trafficke, one with an other, so that it is almost vnpossible for three persons to conuerse together two houres, but they wil fal into talk of one bargaine or another, chopping, changing, or some other kinde of contract. Children, as soone as euer their tongues are at libertie, doe season their sportes with some merchandise or other: and when they goe to schoole, nothing is so common among them as to change, and rechange, buy and sell of that, which they bring from home with them. The Prince with his subiects, the Maister with his seruants, one friend and acquaintance with another, the Captaine with his souldiers, the Husband with his wife, Women with and among themselues, and in a word, all the world choppeth and changeth, runneth and raueth after Marts, Markets and Merchandising, so that all thinges come into Commerce, and passe into traffique (in a manner) in all times, and in all places: not onely that, which nature bringeth forth, as the fruits of the earth, the beasts, and liuing creatures, with their spoiles, skinnes and cases, the metals, minerals, and such like things, but further also, this man maketh merchandise of the workes of his owne handes, this man of another mans labour, one selleth words, another maketh traffike of the skins and bloud of other men, yea there are some found so subtill and cunning merchants, that they perswade and induce men to suffer themselues to bee bought and sold, and we haue seene in our time enow, and too many which haue made merchandise of mens soules.*

* Wheeler, pp. 6, 7. "To make merchandise of men's souls" meant "to preach for money", to be one who can (as Chaucer put it) "wel afile his tongue to win siluer". Thus Bunyan, replying to the Quaker Edward Borrough, in his *A Vindication of Gospel Truths Opened*:

Again to defend thyself thou throwest dirt in my face saying; If we should diligently trace thee, we should find thee in their steps, meaning false prophets, through fained words, through covetousness making merchandise of souls, loving the wages of unrighteousness.

Friend, dost thou speak this as from thy own knowledge, or did any other tell thee so? However, that spirit that led thee out this way, is a lying spirit. For though I be poor, and of no repute in the world, as to outward things; yet through grace I have learned by the example of the apostle to preach the truth; and also to work with my hands, both for my own living, and for those that are with me, when I have opportunity. And I trust that the Lord Jesus, who hath helped me to reject the wages of unrighteousness hitherto, will also help me still, so that I shall distribute that which God hath given me freely, and not for filthy lucre's sake.

In such a social environment it is natural that women should be praised as treasure houses, that self-love should be castigated as unprofitable hoarding, that love itself should be considered a commercial transaction, the lover a merchant, the beloved a desirable commodity; and in such an ethos religion becomes one more ingredient in the mystique of profit and loss. Churchmen become merchants who "trafficke onely for men's soules"; they "make merchandise of prayers by way of exchange"; they advise their congregation to labour busily for grace that "thou maist be as rich a Merchant, have as rich a stocke, and deale in as great and rich Commodities . . . as the richest";* and they make "merchandise of men's souls".[24] Well might a latter-day Moses have complained to his Lord of the English, "Oh, this people have sinned a great sin, and have made them gods of gold."†

The commanding metaphors of Elizabethan love poetry, then, express new but already firmly entrenched beliefs: men have come to believe that hair like gold, teeth like pearls, lips like rubies, and eyes like diamonds or sapphires, are beautiful, conferring their aesthetic approval upon the goddess of conspicuous wealth, "The Venus of the time and state, Pecunia", just as they have come to believe that love itself is a kind of commerce or exchange of riches. As one critic has coyly remarked,

> It may seem *malapropos* to talk about . . . romantic love in terms of buying and selling, leaseholds, merchandise, and bargains, but in each of the early comedies, and in many other plays and poems, Shakespeare wrote of love as of a kind of wealth in which men and women traffic.[25]

---

* The preachers do not reserve the rôle of merchant to those who are (in our own idiom) attempting to 'sell' the true faith. Sampson Price, in *A Heavenly Proclamation to fly Romish Babylon* (1614), refers on several occasions to merchants but always to represent evil-doers, as when he calls priests "the Devils Merchants who in the markets and affaires of the world gaine many soules to hell" (p. 21). This does not reflect a low opinion of merchants, however, it simply reveals the same acceptance of the commercialisation of the spiritual life as that of those who saw themselves as Godly factors and heavenly merchants. It is an acceptance we meet with in Elizabeth's Book of Homilies, in its description of the person who dispenses charity for appearance sake "as a merchant with God" who "doth all for his own gain" (*Certain Sermons or Homilies*, p. 146). In this earlier instance, however, there is a residual medievalism, a tacit presumption that a merchant may be expected to act in the interests of the commonwealth.

† Exodus, xxxii:31. The incident is mentioned in the Book of Homilies as a prime example of idolatry (*Certain Sermons or Homilies*, p. 52); the Israelites, it is there remarked, "made a calf of gold, and kneeled down and worshipped it". Elizabethan love poets are guilty of the same 'idolatry'.

Far from being *malapropos*, the language of Shakespeare is perfectly appropriate to the environment within which his experience of love is rooted; the terms he uses, "of buying and selling, leaseholds merchandise, and bargains", define the very nature of his love.

How could love be defined more truly or more powerfully than in commercial terms in a world in which wealth is revealed like power divine, in which it can

> Make the hoar leprosy ador'd; place thieves,
> And give them title, knee, and approbation,
> With senators on the bench

and in which gold transforms "the wappen'd widow" into a tasty morsel—

> She whom the spital-house and ulcerous sores
> Would cast the gorge at [it] embalms and spices
> To the April day again . . .?[26]

It may well seem *malapropos* of Shakespeare to write of leprosy, thieves and "the wappen'd widow" in terms of adoration and approbation, but the *malapropism* is an essential part of the idiom of a society which makes brothers of impossibilities, in which all natural revulsions submit to wealth and which Jonson epitomised in the remark,

> The honour of it, and the beauty,
> The reputation, ay, and the religion,
> (I was about to say, and had not err'd,)
> Is Queen Pecunia's.[27]

Jonson had not erred in using the word *religion*, recalling its Latin sense of a bond. For a time at least the Elizabethans saw their religious experience in terms which unashamedly expressed the fundamental bonds of their society.

Many Elizabethans were dissatisfied with the new idioms of life. William Smith, writing in 1596, rejects the expensive criterion, "which many writers use", in order to praise his lady-love for her own self:

> Some make their love a goldsmith's shop to be,
> Where orient pearls and precious stones abound:
> In my conceit these far do disagree
> Thy perfect praise of beauty forth to sound.
> O Chloris, thou dost imitate thyself!
> Self's imitating passeth precious stones,
> Or all the Eastern-Indian golden pelf.[28]

Campion also dissociates himself from the commerce of the affections when he declares,

> if we love these ladies, we must give
>   golden showers.
> Give them gold that sell love, give me the nut-brown
>   lass.[29]

But more commonly dissatisfaction with the golden age is revealed in such sentiments as those of Thomas Nashe:

> Rich men, trust not in wealth!
> Gold cannot buy you health,[30]

a remark that is both trite and untrue, for when patients must pay physicians, "gold in physik is a cordial", as Chaucer more truly observed in the lines quoted at the beginning of this section. Contemporary disillusionment, however, showed itself still more commonly in such high-minded other-wordliness as Sidney's,

> Leave me o love, which reachest but to dust,
> And thou my mind aspire to higher things:
> Grow rich in that which never taketh rust,[31]

and Shakespeare's,

> Buy terms divine in selling hours of dross;
> Within be fed, without be rich no more.[32]

But, it will be noticed, even the high-mindedness of a Sidney and a Shakespeare is firmly rooted in the new idioms of life, which insist upon buying and selling and growing rich.

We meet more thoroughgoing disapprovals of the new spirit of the times in the works of Nashe, Dekker, Jonson, and in the more mature Shakespeare, but the full seriousness of their concern cannot be appreciated until the growing totalitarianism of private wealth in the life of Elizabethan England has been recognised. And in order to do this it is necessary to reunderstand the sense in which Elizabeth may be said to have "brought again the Golden Days" and in which the Elizabethan age is indeed "our Golden Age".[33]

5. THE SHAKESPEARIAN DIAGNOSIS

As feudalism lost its grip upon the idioms of life its place was taken by the new normative concerns for expensiveness, profitability and commercial enterprise. It is true that Shakespeare, like many another

Elizabethan poet, casting the lover as thrall or vassal offering service to his lady, still reflects the feudal love ethic in his sonnets and early comedies, but this is as much an archaism as Spenser's Chaucerisms. Times had changed and, as an anonymous poet observed,

> All things with the time do change
> That will not the time obey:
> Some even to themselves seem strange
> Thorough their own delay.[1]

In place of the feudal ethic a new bourgeois ethic had made its appearance, emerging spontaneously from the changed relations of everyday life: so that during the late sixteenth century even such an event as the translation of Ovid becomes something more than an instance of the Renaissance interest in classical literature, for

> Ovid's lusty young men who pursue and his coy young women who resist with reluctance reflect the bargaining and haggling that always goes on over a purchasable commodity.[2]

So that if Ovid's art of love is of more moment than *amour courtois* it is because its attitudes towards the relations of the sexes were more in keeping with the erotic realities of Elizabethan England. It is the transformation of that earlier, courtly code into the mercenary, Ovidian one which is the subject of *Troilus and Cressida*, Shakespeare's diagnosis of the condition of love at the end of the sixteenth century.

The Trojan story came to Shakespeare already coloured by feudal notions of chivalry and courtly love. This is obvious in several passages of the play: in the procession of knights returning from the field, watched by Lady Cressida, and including as the main figure of interest "Brave Troilus! the prince of chivalry" (I.ii); in the argument of the Trojan council scene (II.ii); in Hector's challenge to the Greeks (I.iii) and in his preparation to meet Ajax—when

> The glory of our Troy doth this day lie
> On his fair worth and single chivalry
> (IV.iv.146–7)

—as also in his dismissal of attempts to dissuade him from the day's fighting with the bland assurance,

> I am today i' th' vein of chivalry
> (V.iii.32);

in Diomed's decision to wear Cressida's favour and in his order,

> Go, go, my servant, take thou Troilus' horse;
> Present the fair steed to my Lady Cressida.
> Fellow, commend my service to her beauty;
> Tell her I have chastis'd the amorous Troyan,
> And am her Knight by proof.
>
> (V.v.1–5)

The Trojan story, however, also had a contemporary and local relevance marked in the common and eulogistic description of London as Troynovant, the New Troy. It is thus, for instance, that Whythorne refers to London in a versified account of a trip to the continent:

> From Troinovant I took my kowrs, my cast to Douer strand,
> and fownd A ship which brought mee soon, in Caleiz to tak land. [3]

Turning aside from the inherited character of the story, the distinctively Shakespearian activity in the play is to be found in an emphatic coarsening of the kind of life represented by romance and chivalry. This is most remarkable in the so-called love poetry of the play. Critics have reached such a unanimity of opinion concerning what J. C. Maxwell has called "the genuine intensity of the love poetry" that Mr. Maxwell himself does not feel it necessary to consider the matter,

> because it has never gone unrecognised, whereas the degree to which Shakespeare qualifies our responses to it has often been underestimated. That the love of Troilus, for all the youthful ardour which sometimes tempts us to think of Shakespeare as entirely carried away by it, essentially belongs to the shallow and corrupt world of Troy, is shown also by the arrangement of the scenes. [4]

But, after this rather heretical placing of Troilus's love, Mr. Maxwell returns to received opinion and points out that "in its intensity Troilus's love is very different" from that of Paris and Helen, "who must surely represent the norm of sophisticated love-intrigue at Troy". Apart from the logical oddness of this assertion—the only Trojan love-intrigues are those of Paris and Helen and Troilus and Cressida—it is to be noted that Mr. Maxwell, like many other critics, implicitly accepts the love ethic of Troilus and all that it entails. Bearing in mind how easy it is for all of us to accept current attitudes without appreciating their social implications, this is not altogether surprising: "The field of human relations in Freud's sense is similar to the market" [5] and yet this commonly passes unnoticed because we look upon the world through the same spectacles as Freud. Nonetheless, a certain obtuseness on the part of Shakespearian critics is significant in that it serves as a forcible reminder that we are still in and of a world in which it is natural to view love as a commercial transaction.

In the play itself instances of the coarsening of sensibility which such a view of love involves are so numerous that, unless the above explanation is accepted, it is extremely difficult to understand why they should not have been more generally recognized. In the first scene of the play Troilus defines his evaluation of the love relationship in the oft-quoted lines:

> Tell me, Apollo, for thy Daphne's love,
> What Cressid is, what Pandar, and what we?
> Her bed is India; there she lies, a pearl;
> Between our Ilium and where she resides
> Let it be call'd the wild and wand'ring flood;
> Ourself the merchant, and this sailing Pandar
> Out doubtful hope, our convoy and our bark.
>
> (I.i.97–103)

Addressing Apollo, the god of riches, then, Troilus remarks his own transformation into a merchant for whom Cressida is a desirable commodity and Pandar a trading vessel—elsewhere he describes Pandar as a broker. Later he refers to the more general transformation that has been effected when he seeks to justify the retention of Helen by arguing that she too is a pearl, but one

> Whose price hath launch'd above a thousand ships,
> And turn'd crown'd kings to merchants.
>
> (II.ii.82–3)

Talk about the collapse of feudalism and the rise of capitalism, therefore, is not an impertinence to the play but something to which the text itself draws our attention.

It might be objected that this particular element in the play has an unresolved religious significance, that the characterisation of Troilus as a merchant, the reference to kings turned merchants and to Cressida and Helen as pearls, contains an allusion to Matthew, xiii:45–6:

> Again, the kingdom of heaven is like unto a man that is a merchant seeking goodly pearls: and having found one pearl of great price, he went and sold all that he had and bought it.

Thus Troilus and the crowned kings of Greece turn merchants to seek Helen and Cressida who are goodly pearls. Such an allusion seems probable; the support which it gives to the love ethic of Troilus can be intimated by referring to the following lines from Herbert's poem "The Pearl", which takes Matthew xiii as its text:

> Therefore not sealed, but with open eyes
> I fly to Thee, and fully understand
> Both the main sale and the commodities;
> And at what rate and price I have Thy love.

What Herbert's lines make plain is that the biblical allusion supports rather than detracts from the vision of love as a merchant's venture.

Troilus is a "prince of chivalry", a feudal prince, who has been transformed into a merchant and who, when eventually he must part with Cressida by way of trade, is reduced to the commercially-minded lament,

> We two, that with so many thousand sighs
> Did buy each other, must poorly sell ourselves.
>
> (Iv.iv.38–9)

But the consciousness which judges the relationships of men and women by the standards of the market place is not monopolised by Troilus. When Hector has issued his chivalrous challenge to the Greeks, Ulysses takes Nestor to one side and suggests,

> Let us, like merchants, show our foulest wares
> And think perchance they'll sell
>
> (I.iii.359–60)

their "foulest wares" being Ajax, who, according to the too much maligned Thersites, is "bought and sold among those of any wit, like a barbarian slave" (II.i). After his brief encounter with Ajax, Hector is entertained by the Greeks and Achilles desires the opportunity to look him over, "As I would buy thee" (IV.v). In the meantime, Calchas, Cressida's father, pleads with the Greeks that his daughter be procured from Troy as ransom for the captive Trojan Antenor, "he shall buy my daughter" (III.iii). Agreeing to the exchange the Greeks dispatch Diomed to effect it. It is whilst this Grecian broker is waiting in Troy for Cressida to be handed over to him that Paris asks him who really deserves Helen and Diomed proceeds to strip the war of its chivalrous trappings, his opinion being as traditional as that of "the author of the *Elucidarium*, for example, who sees nothing in economic life but the struggle of wolves over carrion".[6]

He merits well to have her that doth seek her,
Not making any scruple of her soilure,
With such a hell of pain and world of charge;
And you as well to keep her that defend her,
Not palating the taste of her dishonour,
With such a costly loss of wealth and friends.
He, like a puling cuckold would drink up
The lees and dregs of a flat tamed piece;
You, like a lecher, out of whorish loins
Are pleas'd to breed out your inheritors.
Both merits pois'd each weighs nor less nor more;
But he as he, the heavier for a whore.

(IV.i.57–68)

Paris, however, is inspired by the same mercenary spirit as Troilus and waves aside Diomed's acid appraisal with a glib,

Fair Diomed, you do as chapmen do,
Dispraise the thing that you desire to buy;
But we in silence hold this virtue well;
We'll not commend what we intend to sell.

(IV.i.77–80)

Plainly, and to avoid labouring the obvious, summarily, such expressions of the nature of love and war reveal a spirit that is neither ancient (Greek or Trojan) nor medieval (romantic or chivalrous) but Elizabethan-Jacobean as portrayed by John Wheeler,[7] in short, the spirit of capitalism.

The coarsening of life associated with this spirit is implicit, then, in the use of commercial idioms to define, amongst other things, the nature and dignity of love. That Shakespeare's use of such a language is deliberate requires no external evidence. The coarseness that finds its natural expression in the vocabulary of trade is evident in the character of the love poetry. In the opening and, according to Shakespearian practice, directive scene of the play Troilus is impatient with the delay in procuring a meeting with Cressida and protests to Pandar:

I tell thee I am mad
In Cressid's love. Thou answer'st 'She is fair'—
Pour'st in the open ulcer of my heart—
Her eyes, her hair, her cheek, her gait, her voice,
Handlest in thy discourse. O, that her hand,
In whose comparison all whites are ink
Writing their own reproach; to whose soft seizure

> The cygnet's down is harsh, and spirit of sense
> Hard as the palm of ploughman!
>
> (I.i.50–8)

It takes Shakespeare only fifty lines to reach this point, a point at which we already notice the predicament in which Troilus is involved; he is torn between what he is capable of imagining and what he feels capable of enacting. We are made especially aware of this gap by the disjunction of feeling marked by the expression "soft seizure". This disjunction serves to create a gulf between what can be handled in 'discourse' or imagination and what Troilus later refers to as "the capacity of [his] ruder powers". But it is the *character* of Troilus's imagination that defines the quality of his 'love' poetry: the sensual anticipation of 'handlest' becomes an anticipated rape in "soft seizure" and a recognition that the "spirit of sense" will prove incapable of distilling the fullest enjoyment out of the imagined situation.*

Troilus returns to his predicament when left alone to soliloquise in Act III, scene ii:

> I am giddy; expectation whirls me round.
> Th'imaginary relish is so sweet
> That it enchants my sense; what will it be
> When that the wat'ry palate tastes indeed
> Love's thrice-repured nectar?—Death, I fear me;
> Swooning distraction; or some joy too fine,
> Too subtle-potent, tun'd too sharp in sweetness,
> For the capacity of my ruder powers.
>
> (III.ii.17–24)

Here he is again thrown off balance ("I am giddy; expectation whirls me round", cf. "I tell thee I am mad") by the realisation that the capacity of his "ruder powers", his senses, sets a limit to the enjoyment he can hope to get out of the physical possession of Cressida and it is characteristic that such a natural limitation should appear to him to be, as he tells Cressida, monstrous:

> This is the monstruosity in love, lady, that the will is infinite, and the execution confin'd; that the desire is boundless, and the act a slave to limit.
>
> (III.ii.78–80)

---

* For a naïver view see David Kalstone, "Sir Philip Sidney: The Petrarchan Vision" in *Elizabethan Poetry: Modern Essays in Criticism* ed. Paul J. Alpers (Oxford, 1967), pp. 188–9. Kalstone believes that such passages express "the boundless desires and expectations of wonder embodied in Petrarchan rhetoric"!

The act, it will be noticed, is invariably one of touch and taste, an act of handling, seizing, of relishing with the palate, a motion firmly circumscribed by the "spirit of sense" and the capacity of the "ruder powers". Thus, in the opening scene of the play, Troilus and Pandar discuss the wooing of Cressida in terms of the preparation of a cake and when, towards the end of the play, she passes to Diomed, Troilus remarks that only

> The fractions of her faith, orts of her love,
> The fragments, scraps, the bits and greasy relics
> Of her o'er-eaten faith, are bound to Diomed.
>
> (V.ii.156–8)

He almost invariably thinks of Cressida with his belly; beginning as a tasty titbit yet to be enjoyed she ends as a piece of left-over meat. The sentiment of these last lines is inherent in the characterisation of Troilus. Already in the council scene (II.ii) he has found it apposite to liken Helen to left-over meat; he argues there that she should not be returned to the Greeks because

> the remainder viands
> We do not throw in unrespective sieve,
> Because we now are full.
>
> (II.ii.70–2)

In the reply of Diomed to Paris, which has already been quoted, we are offered an appraisal of Helen remarkably similar to those which Troilus makes of Helen and Cressida. According to Diomed, Agamemnon is prepared to "drink up The lees and dregs of a flat tamed piece", Helen, whom Diomed later describes as 'carrion'. The point of this observation is that the spirit which emerges in the characterisation of Troilus is not simply a piece of characterisation. The figure of Troilus, as has been seen in his use of the vocabulary of trade, expresses the central preoccupations of the play. The Greeks, in the figure of Achilles, share the debility of Troilus:

> Imagin'd worth
> Holds in his blood such swol'n and hot discourse
> That 'twixt his mental and his active parts
> Kingdom'd Achilles in commotion rages,
> And batters down himself.
>
> (II.iii.167–71)

However, where in Troilus the disjunction of imagination and action arises from lust, in Achilles it derives from self-love, or pride. And as Troilus's passion is defined as the grossest of belly-appetites, so too is the pride of the Greeks, Ajax and Achilles; Ulysses remarks of them,

> How one man eats into another's pride,
> While pride is fasting in his wantonness!
> (III.iii.136–7)

But the whole of the play is busily reducing life to the demands of the belly: not only pride—"He that is proud eats up himself" (II.iii.150)— but lechery—"lechery eats itself" (V.iv.34)—reputation—

> The Troyans taste our dear'st repute
> With their fin'st palate
> (I.iii.337–8)

advice—

> I begin to relish thy advice;
> And I will give a taste thereof forthwith
> To Agamemnon
> (I.iii.388–90)

grief—

> The grief is fine, full, perfect, that I taste,
> . . .
> If I could temporize with my affection
> Or brew it to a weak and colder palate,
> The like allayment could I give my grief
> (Iv.iv.3–8)

and love—

> He eats nothing but doves, love; and that breeds hot blood, and hot blood begets hot thoughts, and hot thoughts beget hot deeds, and hot deeds is love.
> (III.i.122–4)

And Diomed, it will be remembered, scorns Paris for "Not palating the taste" of Helen's dishonour. Further quotation would be tedious, but these few examples serve to make the point that Ulysses's contention that 'appetite' is "a universal wolf" (I.iii) touches the very quick of Shakespeare's traditionalist conception of the spirit of capitalism as a force which reduces life to a mere satisfaction of the appetites.

For it was of the essence of trade to drag into a position of solitary prominence the acquisitive appetites; and towards these appetites, which to most modern thinkers have seemed the one sure social dynamic, the attitude of the medieval theorist was that of one who holds a wolf by the ears.[8]

The extent of this traditional concern can be seen when Troilus, chafing against the natural limitations of his appetites, his senses, touches upon the subject of time. Critics have made it abundantly clear that time has a special significance in the play; that this is superficial is apparent when Troilus, on parting with Cressida, expands upon the theme of *tempus fugit*:

> Injurious time now with a robber's haste
> Crams his rich thievery up, he knows not how.
> As many farewells as be stars in heaven,
> With distinct breath and consign'd kisses to them,
> He fumbles up into a loose adieu,
> And scants us with a single famish'd kiss,
> Distasted with the salt of broken tears.
>
> (IV.iv.41–7)

The thematic function of time here is simply to define the sensibility of Troilus and, consequently, that of the play: time is appetitive, sensual and limiting—Time with "haste Crams his rich thievery up . . . And scants us with a single famish'd kiss, Distasted"; more especially, Time is lecherous—"He fumbles up into a loose adieu"; there can be little doubt as to the dominant sense of the ambiguous word 'loose' (cf. "loose woman"). The association between time and Troilus is not circumstantial; the lines above bring together the gluttonous anticipation of the passage from Act III, scene ii, "I am giddy; expectation whirls me round", and the implicit lecherousness of the passage from the opening scene, "I tell thee I am mad" (compare, for instance, "Handlest in thy discourse" with "He fumbles up into a loose adieu").

Something of the failure of vision in accepting naïve romantic accounts of Troilus, such as that of Professor Wilson Knight in *The Wheel of Fire* or that of Dr. Tillyard, who saw him as "a romantic and unfortunate lover",[9] should by now be apparent. It is inordinately difficult, at least when reading the play, to understand where Mr. Maxwell finds any intensity in the love of Troilus, or rather any love in the intensity of Troilus. Of course, Troilus is in contact with the remnants of a chivalrous world, but he is in contact with them as an agent of corruption. It is as such, and certainly not as a chivalrous lover,

that Troilus desires access to Cressida, as must be obvious to the most
romantically biased reader when Troilus begs Pandar,

> O, be thou my Charon,
> And give me swift transportation to those fields
> *Where I may wallow in the lily beds*
> Propos'd for the deserver!
> (III.ii.10–13. My italics)

The real nature of the disjunction between action and imagination in
Troilus is made explicit in the lines just quoted, in his conception of the
love relationship. Love to Troilus is the relationship between his own
capacity for pig-like defilement (to 'wallow')—his "ruder powers", his
"spirit of sense"—and what he imagines to be the delicate purity ("the
lily beds") of Cressida—"love's thrice repured nectar", "In whose
comparison all whites are ink" and "The cygnet's down is harsh". And
Troilus, with his mercenary-mindedness and appetitiveness, is but an
abstract of the corruptive spirit which the play as a whole is 'about'.

The corruption of contemporary life did not escape attention in the
sixteenth century; social ills were commonly recognised as pathological
conditions of the body politic. Caroline Spurgeon has pointed out, for
instance, that in *Hamlet* "the idea of an ulcer or tumour, as descriptive
of the unwholesome condition of Denmark morally, is, on the whole,
the dominating one".[10] In the mid-1530's Thomas Starkey complains
of the "sickness and grievous diseases in our politic body".[11] Later in
the century Armigail Waad, in a memorandum probably intended for
Cecil, remarks that "I do here grossly fashion our commonweal, sick
or diseased"* and considers the growth in wealth and power of the

---

* "The Distresses of The Commonwealth, With The Means to Remedy Them", reptd.
in Henry Gee, *The Elizabethan Prayer-Book and Ornaments* (1902) App. III, pp. 206–15.
Edwin Sandys, *Sermons* (1585), remarked,

> It is commonly saide that the common wealth is sore diseased, and that everie member of
> that body seemeth to be grieved. Remedie would bee sought in time, least remedie came
> too late. But I am no Phisition for that bodie, and therefore it is not fit for me to
> minister any medicine to it.
>
> (Quoted in Helen White, p. 178.)

The Church was seen in the same way:

> For lyke as by reason that the partes of mans body are naturally knytte and joyned
> togyther eche to other therefore if one of theym be greved the other also feleth grefe:
> even so we that are members of Chrystes mistycall body joyned by faythe and charyte
> ought wyllyngly and mercyfully to offre help to such as have nede.

William Marshall, trans., *The Forme and Maner of Subvention or Helping for Pore People
Devysed and Practysed i the Cytie of Hypres in Flanders* (1535). (Quoted in Helen White,
p. 256.)

middle class as one of the chief causes of social sickness: in Jonson's words,

> These possess wealth, as sick men possess fevers,
> Which trulier might be said to possess them.[12]

It is in such pathological terms that Shakespeare fashions the corruption of life in *Troilus and Cressida*. Troilus refers to his desire as "the open ulcer" of his heart in the opening scene and in the council scene Hector puts down the persuasions of Troilus and Paris to "the hot passion of distempered blood" and warns Troilus that

> the will dotes that is attributive
> To what infectiously itself affects.
> (II.ii.58–9)

Although Troilus does not accept this diagnosis, the symptoms he reveals a little later demonstrate its veracity:

> My heart beats thicker than a feverous pulse;
> And all my powers do their bestowing lose.
> (III.ii.35–6)

And the sickening quality of his passion—sickness is a prominent feature in the language of Troilus's love poetry—assumes almost Hamletesque proportions in lines such as those which commend the keeping of Helen:

> We turn not back the silks upon the merchant
> When we have soil'd them: nor the remainder viands
> We do not throw in unrespective sieve
> Because we now are full.
> (II.ii.69–72)

Actual vomiting is strongly suggested in the last two lines. Troilus is thrusting forth his own sick view of Helen as good reason. His nausea surges up again when confronted with Cressida's defection:

> The fractions of her faith, orts of her love,
> The fragments, scraps, the bits, and greasy relics
> Of her o'er-eaten faith are bound to Diomed.
> (V.ii.155–7)

It is, of course, Troilus who has played the glutton throughout, Troilus who has "o'er-eaten", and, clinging to the belief that lily beds can be wallowed in without defiling their purity, he regurgitates the truth for which he has no stomach.

F

According to the diagnosis of their complaint, offered to the Greeks by Ulysses, each Greek,

> sick
> Of his superior, grows to an envious fever
> Of pale and bloodless emulation
> And 'tis this fever that keeps Troy on foot.
>
> (I.iii.132–5)

The metaphor upon which Shakespeare is relying is not immediately apparent. The plague is mentioned frequently, but this is not very precise. Thersites is always at hand to damn the Greeks and Trojans alike with the plague and to speculate upon its effect in repulsive detail:

> Agamemnon—how if he had boils full, all over, generally? . . .
> And those boils did run—say so. Did not the general run then?
> Were not that a botchy core? . . . Then there would come some
> matter from him . . .
>
> (II.i.2–9)*

But the disease is closely associated with the appetites and infects the blood and only gradually makes its presence felt. And it is only gradually, as one approaches the end of the play, that the venereal nature of the infection is made more specific. The suppressed metaphor comes to the surface in Thersite's reference to the Neapolitan bone ache, a reference taken up by Pandar in the epilogue when he begs "A goodly medicine for my aching bones" and bequeathes his diseases to "Brethren and sisters of the hold-door trade".

The play draws to an end on an almost apocalyptic note with Troilus invoking the gods:

> Sit, gods, upon your thrones, and smite at Troy.
> I say at once let your brief plagues be mercy,
> And linger not our sure destruction on!
>
> (V.ix.7–9)

It is a vision of disease and destruction which Pandar expands in his epilogue.

---

* Although Thersite's language is repulsive, the sixteenth century had a strong stomach. His words are very similar to those used by John Fisher in his commentary on the second penitential psalm:

As we se a byle or botche full of matter and fylth the more and the lenger it be hyd, the more groweth the corrupcyon and venemouse infeccyon of it, and also perceth to the bones and corrupteth them.

John Fisher, *English Works*, i (E.E.T.S. London, 1876), p. 27.

The epilogue is addressed to members of Pandar's guild, those that are "of Pandar's hall", namely, 'traders' and 'bawds', "Good traders in the flesh", "Brethren and sisters of the hold-door trade"—within the play, to those who have been revealed to us as "Good traders in the flesh", Troilus, Paris, Diomed, Ulysses, Calchas, Nestor, etc. Pandar acknowledges and bemoans their lot:

> O traders and bawds, how earnestly are you set a work, and how ill requited!
>
> (V.x.37)

Their only reward is incurable disease—encroaching blindness ("Your eyes, half out") and "aching bones"—and final destruction:

> Some two months hence my will shall here be made.
> . . .
> Till then I'll sweat and seek about for eases,
> And at that time bequeath you my diseases.
>
> (V.x.51-5)

The dramatic irony of the epilogue's complaint hardly requires comment. The epilogue fitly concludes the play's exploration and definition of that transformation of life, specifically of romantic love and chivalrous war, that was being effected by emergent capitalism.

The distinctively Shakespearian activity in the play, then, assesses the weakening of feudal relations that had taken place during the sixteenth century by bringing to bear upon a world of romance and chivalry (the world of the Trojan war as presented by medieval and Elizabethan writers) the powers of personal and social corruption inherent in the spirit of capitalism. Shakespeare's definition of this spirit in terms of the appetites belongs to that medieval conception of social life which viewed the appetites as necessary but subservient to what was distinctively human in life, expressing as they did man's animal as opposed to his human nature. Shakespeare, therefore, implicitly condemns the reduction of life to the pursuit of animal satisfactions because it *is* a reduction, depressing life to a level at which gluttony and lechery become its dominant qualities and devoting man to the demands of his appetites and the means to satisfy them, as Troilus is devoted to Cressida and Dekker's thrifty citizen is devoted to gold.

In the play, Shakespeare's implicit conception of society is that of medieval humanism. Society is a super-individual, it is the body politic with a head, members, and all the other components, with their various functions, analogous to the constitution of a person. So it is that in a society such as that observed by John Wheeler, where human activity is directed by the demands of the appetites, terms such as 'gluttony' and 'lechery', which we would use in judgment of an individual, serve as terms of political appraisal, applying to the state of that super-individual, the body politic. Social analysis, therefore, such as that of Starkey, Waad and Shakespeare, often takes the form of a medical diagnosis, which a twentieth-century reader may understand metaphorically. For many Elizabethans, however, the use of such apparently personal terms as 'disease', 'gluttony', 'lechery', although ambiguous was not metaphoric—to them society *was* a gigantic individual with all of an individual's characteristics. It is in the ambiguity of this essentially medieval cast of mind that Shakespeare's political humanism lies and in *Troilus and Cressida* we can appreciate its power and integrity not in spite of but because of its limitations.

In the play, the body politic of medieval social theory has become a creature of appetite, "a universal wolf" to use Ulysses's phrase, afflicted with the incurable diseases that follow in the wake of over-indulgence, and therefore doomed to eventual death. The integrity of this use of medieval social theory can be appreciated if it is borne in mind that the theory reflects medieval social life, feudalism; that form of living had been corrupted and was doomed. The limitation, on the other hand, is that such a view of society, being rigidly feudal, does not allow of any perception of new forms of social growth. Today we can see that out of a coarse and vulgar appetitiveness arose a new respect for man's material well-being and out of sensual curiosity arose modern science.

An anonymous reviewer in *The Times Literary Supplement* has quoted this last sentence as "a very serious qualification" of what I have been saying of *Troilus and Cressida* and has asked the old question, "Should it not in honesty be added that, for good or bad, Marxism arose from this 'villainy' too?"[13]

A Marxist does not believe, as did Andrew Marvell, that

> 'Tis Madness to resist or blame
> The force of angry Heaven's flame,

for although it may be irresistible it is none the less deplorable that the price of social progress should be the denial of a humane existence to countless people. Had the well-to-do of the eighteenth century taken heed of Pope and followed the benevolent example of the Man of Ross the condition of the 'common' people of England would have been more bearable than it was. But it was only the avariciousness of the well-to-do which enabled the accumulation of wealth that made possible the industrial revolution. The industrial revolution in turn only succeeded because of the brutal exploitation of men, women and children. The consequence of that revolution is the more humane existence enjoyed by the 'common' people of England today. Is the existence we now enjoy to be offered as "a very serious qualification" of the inhuman conditions under which so many people lived and worked in the eighteenth and the nineteenth centuries? To believe that such conditions were necessary to our own more comfortable and enlightened existence is not to approve them nor to pretend that they were any less vicious and brutal than they were. Marxism, nevertheless, has always emphasised the fact that capitalism was a prodigious step forward in the development of human society, but it has never slurred over the tragic content of human development in class society. Marxism arose not out of capitalism but out of a perception of the tragic human limitations imposed by it. It is some of those limitations that Shakespeare exposes in *Troilus and Cressida*; he does so by concentrating attention upon an area of life, and that the most intimately human, in which the spirit of capitalism works without hope of redemption, like a kind of diabolic grace. "Love", as D. H. Lawrence observed, "is no deal, nor merchant's bargaining",[14] that is, prostitution.

3

The Art of Being Human: Literature in the Seventeenth Century

I. THE LITTLE WORLD OF JOHN DONNE

Troilus and Cressida presents Shakespeare in an unusually Swiftian mood. It falls short of greatness because it creates a vision of disintegration and doom unrelieved by an intimation of a more humane existence. This may seem a naïve objection to its artistic success, but the contention that the supremely creative act realises the values of an integrated life is widely accepted. We have come to recognise that for all his intelligent analysis Donne's true greatness lies in his capacity to integrate what we, in the normal course of things, too readily accept as disparate. This valuation rests upon the supposition that our lives, our experiences of life, are generally not of an integrated kind, are not whole. Suggested in this view is the belief that the power of man to draw the world into direct relationship to himself is not as strong in us as it should be. Contrary to common belief, therefore, what the supremely creative act implicitly reveals is not the genius required to overcome the recalcitrance of the world, but the magnetic power of man made whole and concentric to himself.

The creative act is one which constitutes man whole, it establishes and defines man's real self. The compelling rightness with which Donne unites apparent disparities instances not only the supremely creative act but also man's ability to establish his own relatedness, to overcome his own estrangement. Another way of putting this would be to say that the creative act is one by which man answers the demand of the Delphic oracle, "Know thyself", and defines his self by establishing his true relationship to nature and to other men.

In the practical world in which the creative act takes place the establishment of one's relationship to nature and the establishment of one's relationship to others are not separable actions but complementary aspects of the discovery of human naturalness. Thus if we wish to define the sense in which Wordsworth is a truly creative poet we do so not with reference to the philosophic pretensions of such a poem as *The Prelude*, not, that is, generally and intellectually, but specifically, by examining the real medium in which Wordsworth humanised nature and naturalised humanity, the actual passages and poems in which he realised his haunting consciousness of the fact that nature exists for man "as a bond with man", as "the life-element of the human world".[1] It is in similar terms, in terms of its attempt to create a human world, that one ultimately distinguishes the poetry of Donne from that which we usually think of as Elizabethan. His historical achievement was to promote that language of the mind "wheare in the soule . . . ffeelethe the sensis" (as Wyatt expressed it)[2] and so to join Jonson in displacing the idioms of the market place from their commanding position in poetry.

The high reputation which Donne enjoyed in his own time, and which is on record in such poems on Donne as those of Jonson and Carew, suffered an eclipse following the Restoration, an eclipse which lasted until the present century. During the twenties not only did his poetry rise in the estimation of the critics, but it also influenced that of many younger poets and Donne was lost in a modernity which was perhaps a more serious threat to his true standing and importance than the centuries of neglect. The complex intelligence of his poetry was too readily associated with the querulous metaphysics of Eliot and the trendy intellectual posturing of Auden. What was in danger of being lost to view was that real quality and strength which is so distinctive of Donne and which derives from a view of the world which is medieval rather than modern.

Perhaps the commonest assertion of Donne's poetry is that summed up in the line, "I am a little world made cunningly".[3] It is a conceit to which, in various forms, the poetry continuously returns:

> My face in thine eye, thine in mine appeares,
> And true plaine hearts doe in the faces rest,
> Where can we finde two better hemispheares
> Without sharpe North, without declining West?
>   ("The Good-morrow")

> You, to whom love was peace, that now is rage;
> Who did the whole worlds soule contract, and drove
>   Into the glasses of your eyes,
>   So made such mirrors, and such spies,
> That they did all to you epitomize
>   ("The Canonization")

> This flea is you and I, and this
> Our marriage bed, and marriage temple is;
> Though parents grudge, and you, we're met,
> And cloystered in these living walls of Jet.
>
> ("The Flea")[4]

In other poems a little room becomes an everywhere and a tear becomes a world. The central, organising conceit here is that which miniaturises everything and contracts the matter of experience into the small circumference of a face, an eye, a flea, a tear, a little room.

Thus, although Donne's knowledge and his curiosity are far-ranging, they are contracted and constrained within a narrow compass; they are formed into the innumerable images of a little, closed world in which the mind, though freely-ranging, moves in circles. In *The Good Morrow* the attention moves from the lovers, "thou and I", to the little room, to the new worlds of the sea-discoverers, to "worlds on worlds", to the world of the lovers, and so finally returns to the lovers, "thou and I". The famous compasses image in *A Valediction: Forbidding Mourning* has, therefore, a significance in Donne's poetry that has not often been perfectly understood. Of all Donne's images it is the one which most succinctly describes the movement and the shape of Donne's mind and attention.

In his *Devotions* Donne uses a rather different image to represent his vision of the world and describes the universe as "Nature's nest of boxes" in which "The Heavens contain the earth, the earth, cities, cities, men. And all these are concentrique."[5] There is, however, no substantial difference between this and the other images I have been describing. I mention the circle as the organising image of Donne's mind, as of his poetry, because it occurs more commonly in his poetry than does any other image; like the box, the circle is considered a closed container. The circle was held by the medieval schoolmen to be the perfect shape; and when their vision of the universe is considered this is not surprising. The universe itself was seen as a system of nine concentric spheres; time was measured in the common mind, as it was experienced, not in terms of linear progression but in terms of the cycle of the seasons; the life of man, divided into its seven stages, began and ended in childhood, and death itself was, in the words of *Epithalamion at Lincolns Inne*, "A grave, but, to a better state, a cradle"; the intellectual life of man was governed by the dialectic and by deductive logic, which returns to the premises from which it sets out. Even the divisions of religious opinion are thought of by Donne as "connatural pieces of one circle", as he expresses it in a letter to Sir H. R.[6] So that when Columbus set out for the East by sailing to the West he was simply being more consistent than those who ridiculed him, and when Drake circumnavigated the globe his voyage was a perfect emblem (as Donne might have called it) of the circling mind exploring the closed universe. It is the effect of this shaping vision of existence that informs Donne's work with its organising images of circularity: the worlds, globes, eyes, spheres, and coins; the circumambulating leg of the compasses; the movement west in search of the east in *Good Friday: Riding Westwards*.

Naturally, such a vision not only gives rise to paradoxes—How can a man travel east by going west? asked Columbus's critics. How can all be nothing? asked the schoolmen. But that same vision enables such paradoxes to be resolved: a man can travel east by going west because the world is a globe and all can be nothing because the figure o represents a sphere and a zero. Such conundrums compose some part of what too commonly passes for Donne's wit; they remind us that the closed and circular world of medieval thought and experience was a paradoxical place. In such a world everything could become its opposite or contrary, east could become west, age become childhood, death become birth, for it touches the resurrection (as Donne expresses it), and one small room becomes an everywhere. This is a world in which, as Donne observes in the sermon on Cockayne, "there is no acquiescence, but a vicissitudinary transmutation into one another".[7]

This, then, is a world of riddles and at times explicitly recognised as such in Donne's poetry, as in *The Canonization*, with its declaration that

> The Phoenix ridle hath more wit
> By us, we two being one, are it[8]

and in the assertion of *Lovers Infiniteness* that

> Love's riddles are, that though thy heart depart,
> It stayes at home, and thou with losing sav'st it.[9]

The logic involved in such paradoxes is that of the scholastic dialectic, the logic of the circular world: the tear contains the world and the world contains the tear; the All is contained in the One and the One in the All. This paradoxical principle, deriving from the imagined structure of the universe, establishes all contradictions as truths, because everything is both itself and its opposite: Christ is pure and he is a ravisher, in *Batter my heart, three-person'd God*, and one can only retain one's purity by being ravished and can only become free by being enthralled:

> Take mee to you, imprison mee, for I
> Except you' enthrall mee, never shall be free,
> Nor ever chast, except you ravish mee.[10]

This kind of riddling wit is not only that of the poems, of course, it is also that of the *Certaine Paradoxes and Problemes*, a work which is truly juvenilia not because the intellectual methods employed lack maturity but because of the impish frivolity with which they are employed.

The impression received from these juvenile productions is of one intent upon ridiculing orthodox methods of reasoning by bringing them to bear upon inconsequential matters. It is as though Donne is producing a skit upon such a "disputation of Schoolmen" as that to which he refers in his *Problemes*; his "Why did the Divell Reserve Jesuites till These Latter Dayes?" appearing to be a satirical counterpart of the schoolmen's "why the Divell could not make lice in Aegypt".[11] And because there is more than a strain of this intellectual skittishness in the use of orthodox dialectic and ratiocination in Donne's work, it might be concluded that he pokes fun at the gyrations of the mind as it explores the closed medieval universe. But this, I think, is where we need to distinguish between Donne as a wag and Donne as a wit. It is by no means always evident that those who have written of Donne and who have quite rightly stressed the importance of his wit have seen the distinction between wit and puckishness in his work. Donne is obviously being puckish when, in the *Problemes*, he concludes that Puritans make long sermons because "It is their duty to preach on till their Auditory wake"[12] and when he suggests that common opinion has afforded souls to women in order to convince us "that sith a woman hath a soule, a soule is no great matter".[13] He is indulging in the same waggishness when he concludes *Loves Alchymie* with the advice,

> Hope not for minde in women; at their best
> Sweetnesse and wit, they'are but *Mummy*, possest.[14]

Now obviously this sort of thing is quite funny—as long as you don't happen to be a Puritan or a woman—and in a modern sense of the word it could be called witty; but is it the wit which has earned Donne the reputation he now enjoys or that to which Carew was referring when he awarded to Donne the universal monarchy of wit?[15] Surely not. What is generally considered to be important in Donne's work is not his waggishness and not the fun he pokes at intellectual orthodoxy. On the contrary, Donne's wit and peculiar strength appears to derive directly from a mind and an imagination which has made itself very much at home within the confines of a closed world.

It is, of course, difficult to define that quality which Donne and his contemporaries would have called 'wit'. But it is also difficult to define that quality which we call 'intelligence'. However, this should not worry us unduly: we can distinguish intelligence even if we have some difficulty in defining it. There is one thing we can safely say of Donne's wit and that is that it is a kind of insight into the relationships of things. Furthermore, if we look carefully at its *modus operandi*, it appears to be an insight into the psychological relationships of man to the world about him. For instance, in *A Valediction: Of Weeping*[16] Donne's conceit establishes an analogical connection between tears, coins, globes and worlds, and such a connection (as has already been remarked) reflects a traditional way of looking at things. Donne's special contribution is the perception that by diminishing the scale of the Ptolemaic spheres it becomes possible to establish a psychological condition as a reasonable fact. For the poem is ultimately concerned with the tendency of men to translate their emotional condition into a universal one: when you're smiling the whole world smiles with you, when you're depressed the whole world becomes depressing, or as Donne's expresses it, "thy tears mixt with mine doe overflow This World". Once you accept Donne's analogies as reasonable insights, then this psychological condition becomes a reasonable fact rather than a pathetic fallacy. And if one accepts the medieval view of the world, then Donne's analogies do appear reasonable even if they are strange and new.

Now it may be argued that although Donne's wit, his insight into the relations of things, constitutes the real foundation of his poetic achievement, nevertheless this insight can hardly be accepted as an adequate one. One can imagine someone arguing, for instance, that Donne's wit is no more than arid scholasticism and that whilst the old scholastic analogies and dialectic may be brilliant intellectual exercises they are not founded upon any real, or factual, understanding of the world. Donne's analogies, it might be said, are simply elaborate and specious fictions which tell us nothing of the real nature of the world, nothing of the world of fact, and all that we get from the poems, as from scholasticism, is evidence of intellectual ingenuity and agility, admirable enough in itself, perhaps, but hardly profound.

We have already seen a sense in which such a criticism, issuing from a limited conception of the world and of fact, may be said to be beside the point. What Donne does in *A Valediction: Of Weeping* is to define a particular psychological state or disposition in terms of a particular intellectual point of view. The adequacy of this intellectual position is not dependent upon its conformity to some objectively existing reality. Admitting that man sees everything in relationship to himself and that he therefore tends to objectivise his own particular plight, the question is how well suited to expressing this is the intellectual view of the universe relied upon in the *Valediction*? And surely the answer is that it suits very well indeed. No doubt it was with something like this in mind that Eliot remarked in his essay on the metaphysical poets that "A philosophical theory which has entered into poetry is established, for its truth or falsity in one sense ceases to matter, and its truth in another sense is proved."[17] So one would reply to my hypothetical objector that the real profundity of Donne's view of the world, of his philosophical position if you wish, lies in its ability to organise the emotions and render them articulate; in a phrase, to realise the emotional life. One would then go on to point out that Gradgrindery is inadequate not because the 'facts' upon which it prides itself are spurious, but because it lacks this imaginative power. And it is this power, which Donne and his contemporaries frequently referred to as wit, rather than Donne's waggishness, his imagination rather than his fancy, that draws its strength from the medieval vision of the closed and intimate circle of existence.

According to this vision, the whole universe was an image of the human plight and man was seen to be intimately and inextricably connected with every aspect of the universe about him. "The world is a great Volume," remarks Donne in the sermon on Cockayne, "and man the Index of that Booke; Even in the body of man, you may turne to the whole world."[18] It is upon such a perception of the essential relationship between all things which is concentrated in man, that Donne's wit, or imagination, relies. The connections in Donne's work, which Dr. Johnson did not fully appreciate, are not forged by the clever wordplay often implied in labelling his poems conceits, but by this medieval attitude towards human experience, an attitude which places man as an essentially moral animal and the pivot of a morally, or humanly, purposeful universe. The smallest flea and the furthest star alike are, in Gerard Manley Hopkins's phrase, "charged with the grandeur of God". I find this acceptable because, like some modern theologians, I consider God to be a mythopoeic expression of the sublimated life of man. In the *Devotions* Donne refers to "the book of Nature, where though sub-obscurely, and in shadows" God has expressed his own image. On my understanding, the image which man sees obscurely reflected in Nature is his own, an image of his own human nature, and that is why man is "the Index of that Booke" and why "even in the body of man, you may turn to the whole world".[19] In this at least I find myself in agreement with the 'new' theology as represented by John Robinson (one-time Bishop of Woolwich) when he affirmed that the essence of religion is man's relationship to man and to the world about him.[20] This, it seems to me, is the connection prefabricated in that medieval cast of mind which gave to all experience and to all objects of experience the significance of a common purpose, a sublimated human purpose which was believed to be divine. And Donne's so-called disparities are reflections of this medieval unity of outlook, a unity which finds expression in that unity of purpose with which he fuses together the multiplicity of objects impinging upon him and brings it to bear upon a common human centre.

There is, then, an analogy between that moral purpose, which was believed to be omnipresent as a unifying force in the ordering of the universe, and the artistic purpose present as a unifying force in the ordering of Donne's work. In his love poems this is an analogy easily overlooked and yet in them, as throughout his work, Donne implicitly follows the advice tendered in *The Canonization*,

> Beg from above
> A patterne of your love![21]

But, as one might expect, it is in the Divine poems that this analogy is most explicitly recognised. Donne's artistic purpose in *The Crosse*, for instance, imitates that divine purpose which was thought to reveal itself, "though sub-obscurely", even in the most commonplace arrangements and situations:

> Who can deny mee power, and liberty
> To stretch mine armes, and mine owne Crosse to be?
> Swimme, and at every stroake, thou art thy Crosse,
> The Mast and yard make one, where seas do tosse.
> Looke downe, thou spiest out Crosses in small things;
> Looke up, thou seest birds rais'd on crossed wings;
> All the Globes frame, and spheares, is nothing else
> But the Meridians crossing Parallels.[22]

Here the range of images establishes the universal significance of man's crucifixion; the crucifix is the common factor binding together man, bird, small things, ships and globe. At the same time, the crucifixion is made a matter of common experience rather than a remote event in history, for nature itself seems to have taken upon itself the cross as a permanent possibility of human experience. So that here the cross becomes a powerful image drawing upon the range of ordinary experience, an image which knits the man with stretched arms into the pattern of the universe at large, the pattern observed by ship, bird, small things, and globe. And here the point I have been trying to make is firmly established, "thou art thy Cross" and in "the book of Nature" it is your image, man's image, which is reflected.

It is to the creation of this kind of connection between otherwise disparate experiences that we refer when we use the word *wit* to describe the special quality and strength of Donne's work. And it is plainly a connection prefabricated in the medieval view of the world. Man is the centre of this universe, as he stretches out his arms he reveals in doing so new patterns and significances in the world about him. The world is not indifferent to human conduct but intimately related to it. This is an essentially human point of view.

Today, I suppose, we respond to this point of view most readily, or at least most obviously, when it is expressed in exclusively human terms, that is to say, when Donne is referring not to the connections between man and the rest of the world, but when he is referring specifically to relationships between people, as in the most famous passage from the *Devotions*:

> No man is an Island, intire of it selfe; every man is a peece of the Continent, a part of the maine; if a Clod bee washed away by the Sea, Europe is the lesse, as well as if a Promontorie were, as well as if a Manor of thy friends or of thine owne were; any mans death diminishes me, because I am involved in Mankinde; And therefore never send to know for whom the bell tolls; It tolls for thee.[23]

It is Donne's fundamental perception, that which is realised by his wit and provided to him by the old medieval world picture, that man's relationships to mankind and his relationships to nature are essential aspects of man himself; he stands in relation to the world about him not as an object amongst objects, but as an intrinsic part of one great whole, of which he is the consciousness and centre. Man, in other words, is not set over and against Nature as a spectator or an onlooker;

neither is the individual set over and against the species or society. No man is an island, for his human existence is his social existence, his natural existence as a man. Nature for man, therefore, is essentially human nature, a bond with other men, and man's vision of the world about him is a revelation of his own nature, of the relationships of men within society.

The tightly integrated and closed world of the medieval picture is plainly a reflection of the actual character and organisation of medieval social life. It was to be destroyed by the emergence of a capitalist society, in which men came to be seen as freely competing individuals: and this new individualism produced its own image of the world, in which natural objects appear as things-in-themselves acted upon by powerful external forces—just such a vision as Hobbes has of the social life of man. So, too, incidentally, does Lear. For, in a sense, one might say that Lear rips up the social contract which has kept the viciousness and brutishness of Goneril and Regan in check and in doing so has revealed human nature to be all that Hobbes claims it is in its natural state. Unlike Shakespeare, however, Hobbes has no place in his scheme of things for a Cordelia, for human naturalness as opposed to brutishness. And when that human naturalness which Cordelia represents is rejected and the old focal point of the universe is denied, then it becomes a dogma that there is no necessary connection between the multitudinous objects of the universe, and the vital interconnection of all things, upon which Donne relies, appears at best to be no more than a poetic fiction. Then we say, "Yes, Cordelia is always connected with flowers and Goneril and Regan with vicious animals, but that is only poetic metaphor." For Shakespeare, however, Nature and human nature were not different things; the flowers reflect Cordelia's disposition just as a smile reflects pleasure and the birds on crossed wings reflect the man with stretched arms in Donne's poem *The Crosse*.

2. BEN JONSON AND THE ART OF LIVING

It would be too crude to say that Donne adopts a point of view, because that might suggest a deliberated act, when what actually happens is that his poetry and prose realise a certain inclination and commitment of the mind and sensibility. Like Donne's, Jonson's poetry and prose are inclined and committed to a traditional point of view and a traditional set of values, although these are not the same as those which we encounter in reading Donne. Whereas Donne's work reflects certain assumptions concerning the structure of the universe,

Jonson's work relies upon a more explicitly social and less obviously metaphysical commitment.

Jonson's artistic consciousness is not only thoroughly social, however, it is also profoundly conservative; as Mr. Bamborough has pointed out, "the whole tenor of his life and work suggests that he has a very genuine veneration for established authority".[1] His aims and intentions as an artist are intimately connected to his own estimation of popular needs and he would doubtless maintain that it was to the credit of his art that it refused to become a Bartholomew or Vanity Fair for the mere titillation of popular fancy. The refusal is at once a matter of artistic principle and of political judgment. This is not to say that Jonson never cast himself in the rôle of popular entertainer, of one by hospitality seeking popular praise. He does so quite openly in the prologue to *The Silent Woman*:

> Truth sayes, of old, the art of making plaies
> Was to content the people; and their praise
> Was to the Poet money, wine, and bayes.
> But in this age, a sect of writers are,
> That, onely, for particular likings care,
> And will taste nothing that is populare.
> With such we mingle neither braines nor brests;
> Our wishes, like to those (make publique feasts)
> Are not to please the cookes tastes, but the guests.[2]

Despite this overture to his audience, however, Jonson is critical of popularity, of what he elsewhere calls "fomie praise, that drops from common jaws",[3] because he is critical of the new life-style which he believed the *hoi polloi* were responsible for creating. In the opening scene of *Volpone*, Volpone and Mosca expose the deformity of the times in a caricature of the "common way" to wealth, with its "mills for yron, Oyle, corne, or men, to grinde 'hem into poulder", its usury, and its readiness to

> Teare forth the fathers of poore families
> Out of their beds, and coffin them, aliue,
> In some kind, clasping prison, where their bones
> May be forth-coming, when the flesh is rotten . . .

The avariciousness of the vulgar, which inspires so many of the plays with a powerful sense of wrong, is complemented in the poems by a positive sense of right, expressed in a vision of feudal benevolence, as in the address *To Penshurst*:

> And though thy walls be of the countrey stone,
> They'are rear'd with no mans ruine, no mans grone,
> There's none, that dwell about them, wish them downe;
> But all come in, the farmer, and the clowne . . .

What are represented are two ways of life; the one self-seeking, mean, avaricious and brutal, the other sociable, hospitable, generous and humane. The plays hold a reproving mirror up to the one, "a mirror, As large as is the stage whereon we act",[4] whilst the poems, and to some extent the masques, celebrate the other.

This political vision is not unique to Jonson, any more than Shakespeare's old-world metaphysics are unique to Shakespeare; what is unique, in both cases, is the power and finesse with which the vision is realised. No other Elizabethan or Jacobean can consistently match Jonson in expressing that conformity of artistry to life which is so succinctly present in his description of the son he has produced as "Ben. Ionson his best piece of poetrie".[5] The description is something more than a touching testament to his feelings for the child who has died, it is a cryptic summary of his art.

It is precisely because of this conformity that critical judgment is central to any understanding of Jonson. Jonson's world is a world of art, not because he is an aesthete but because he conceives of art as governed by the same standards as those which govern life. This is a recurrent implication of his poetry. In the poem upon Cary and Morison, for example, he praises Morison's fulfilment of his various duties—as soldier, patriot and son—in terms which establish the performance of such duties as an art:

> All Offices were done
> By him, so ample, full, and round,
> In weight, in measure, number, sound.[6]

Words such as *weight, measure, number, sound*, were used, of course, of the art of poetry. In the following stanza of the same poem he refers to the principles of life as to those of a song or air:

> Life doth her great actions spell,
> By what was done and wrought
> In season, and so brought
> To light: her measures are, how well
> Each syllab'e answer'd, and was form'd, how faire;
> These make the lines of life, and that's her ayre.

Such lines make it quite evident in what sense Jonson's art is the art of living and illustrate quite well the manner in which comments upon life assume the character of literary judgments. It is this conception of art which informs his poetry, even when it is not so obviously alluding to art, as in such lines from the poem to Cary and Morison as those which maintain that

> In small proportions, we just beautie see:
> And in short measures, life may perfect bee.

Here, words such as *proportions* and *measures* are not borrowed from art —in the poem they refer to the size and shape and to the span of life of natural objects—nevertheless, the lines are as pertinent to Jonson's view of art as they are to his view of life; that life is finest, as that art is best, which observes due measure and proportion.

If this attitude to perfection, as something defined by *measure* and *proportion*, suggests a classical approach to art, and life, this is hardly surprising: Jonson's admiration and emulation of the poets of ancient Greece and, more especially, ancient Rome, is well known. He adopts the view that art and life require a disciplined effort for their proper fulfilment; a classical stance well attested in Jonson's praise of Shakespeare for his "well turned, and true-filed lines"[7] and in his reply to those who applauded Shakespeare because he never deleted a line, "would he had blotted a thousand".[8] If we may caricature romanticism by saying that it assumes that poetry should be "the spontaneous overflow of powerful feelings",[9] Jonson's classicism may be expressed in the contrary opinion "that he, who casts to write a liuing line, must sweat", which we find in the poem on Shakespeare. In short, measure and proportion in a properly ordered life, as in the "well turned, and true-filed lines" of art, is the result of application and effort.

This perception of the importance of measure, proportion and discipline to Jonson's conception of art and life, however, is not that associated with high formality and rigidity; the disciplined effort is that required for ease and negligence—as Pope remarks, "True ease in writing comes from art not chance."[10] The achievement desired is that of simplicity, freedom and the appearance of natural negligence; it is that described in Clerimont's Song from *The Silent Woman* (I.i):

> Give me a looke, give me a face,
> That makes simplicitie a grace;
> Robes loosely flowing, hair as free:

> Such sweet neglect more taketh me,
> Than all th'adulteries of art.
> They strike mine eyes, but not my heart.

It is typical of Jonson's work that ideals of art should find such a natural expression as ideals of life, or rather that the ideals expressed should be equally applicable to art and life.

The conception of art, which I have been trying to describe, is strongly informed by a sense of values, by beliefs which place art amidst the normal civilities of life. In *Inviting a Friend to Supper* the friend is tempted not only by the offer of good food and drink, but by the promise of good literature and a chance to discuss it whilst feasting:

> my man
> Shall reade a piece of Virgil, Tacitus,
> Livie, or of some better booke to us,
> Of which we'll speake our minds, amidst our meate.

Good literature and conversation take their place with ease amidst the partridge, woodcock, pheasant and canary wine, as ingredients of a civility which is marked by friendship, hospitality and generosity. So that in insisting that Jonson is classical in spirit, is civil and mannered, it is necessary to elucidate what is actually meant by civility and manners, and this we can do best, I suggest, by referring to the conception of civility and manners which informs such a poem as *Inviting a Friend to Supper*. Just as the classical concern for measure and proportion is not a concern for rigidity and formality, so civility and manners are not associated with formal behaviour and reserve but with good fellowship, generosity and hospitality.

But the values which inform Jonson's art, defining it as an art of living, are most finely realised in the poem *To Penshurst*, a poem which has its antithesis in Pope's description of Timon's villa in the *Epistle to Burlington*. In *To Penshurst* the remarked absence "of polish'd pillars, or a roof of gold", what might be called in the words of Clerimont's Song "th' adulteries of art", is part of the affirmation of the substantial and essential values, what the poem calls the "better markes, of soyle, of ayre, of wood, of water". What the poem so superbly elaborates is a way of life in intimate contact with soil, air, wood and water, which sustain it with their fruitfulness:

> Thy copp's, too, nam'd of *Gamage*, thou has there,
> That never failes to serve thee season'd deere,
> When thou would'st feast, or exercise thy friends.

> The lower land, that to the river bends,
> Thy sheep, thy bullocks, kine, and calves doe feed:
> The middle grounds thy mares, and horses breed.
> Each banke doth yeeld thee coneyes; and the topps
> Fertile of wood, Ashore, and Sydney's copp's,
> To crowne thy open table, doth provide
> The purpled pheasant, with the speckled side:
> The painted partrich lyes in every field,
> And, for thy messe, is willing to be kill'd.
> And if the high swolne Medway faile thy dish,
> Thou hast thy ponds, that pay thee tribute fish,
> Fat, aged carps, that runne into thy net.

Such natural benevolence both sustains and reflects the quality of human life at Penshurst, the interplay of generosity and hospitality between the inhabitants of the house and those "that dwell about them":

> all come in, the farmer, and the clowne:
> And no one empty-handed, to salute
> Thy lord, and lady, though they have no sute.
> Some bring a capon, some a rurall cake,
> Some nuts, some apples; some that thinke they make
> The better cheeses, bring 'hem; or else send
> By their ripe daughters, whom they would commend
> This way to husbands; and whose baskets beare
> An embleme of themselves, in plum, or peare.
> But what can this (more than expresse their love)
> Adde to thy free provisions, farre above
> The neede of such? whose liberall boord doth flow,
> With all, that hospitalitie doth know!
> Where comes no guest, but is allow'd to eate,
> Without his feare, and of the lords owne meate:
> Where the same beere, and bread, and self-same wine,
> That is his Lordships, shall be also mine.

As in *To Penshurst* so in general, Jonson's poetry at its best depends upon a measured response to the fundamental things of human life, to a sense of family and community, to domestic and local pieties, what *To Penshurst* calls "thy Penates" (thy household gods). These make their presence felt obliquely also, in hospitality and good fellowship; so that even the most 'romantic' of the love poems, *Drink to me only*, with its allusion to a toast, suggests conviviality as strongly as it does romance. It is this vision of a proper social life, and not as Mr. Bamborough would have it "his apparent arrogance", which leads Jonson to "his assumption of the rôle of the stern moral critic of his age"[11] and to create a comedy "familiarly allied to the time" wherein we find "the times deformities Anatomiz'd in every nerve and sinew".[12]

Jonson, then, is a classical poet not because as a learned writer with ambitions to become a closet dramatist he is concerned with measure and proportion, decorum, manners, and civilities, but because, like his beloved Horace, his concern for such matters is rooted in a specific sense of human sociability, in a preoccupation with the art of being human. His poetry seeks, in the words of the Horatian *Praises of a Countrie Life*, "To deck the hallow'd Harth", it appeals to the primal human bonds, to "thy Penates", in its sustained sense of superiority to such realistic (i.e. typifying) figures of the age as Mammon and Pecunia.[13] His feeling for nature is a feeling for human naturalness, for that mutual enrichment so finely realised when the *Praises of a Countrie Life* describes the cultivator:

> When that Autumne, through the fields lifts round
> His head, with mellow Apples crown'd,
> How plucking peares, his owne hand grafted had,
> And purple-matching Grapes, hee's glad!

That such lines put one in mind of Marvell and of Keats, the most sensuously rich of all English poets, should be allowed to make its point: when, as in *To Penshurst* and *The Praises of a Countrie Life*, the poetry comes closest to the fundamental values which inspire it, it becomes fuller and richer: the concern for measure and proportion is still there and very much in control, maintaining a tone and rhythm which precludes the kind of sentimentality that mars, say, Victorian feelings for home and family, but measure and proportion are here at work upon a richer substance than they are in other poems.

Such poems are indicative of the true importance of Jonson's concern for measure and proportion; they are essential in defining his attitude towards the great commonplaces: they prevent the local and domestic pieties celebrated in his poetry from being depreciated by sentimentality and sanctimoniousness. The real importance of tone and attitude,[14] measure and proportion, in Jonson's poetry is best illustrated by the *Ode to Himselfe*:

> Come leave the loathed Stage,
> And the more loathsome Age,
> Where pride and impudence in faction knit,

> Usurpe the Chaire of wit:
> Inditing and arraigning every day,
>   Something they call a Play.
>   Let their fastidious vaine
>   Commission of the braine,
> Runne on, and rage, sweat, censure, and condemn,
> They were not made for thee, lesse thou for them.

The poem, incited by the harsh reception of his play *The New Inn*, is deeply flawed by a loss of that balance which is so characteristic of Jonson. In the poem he puffs up his own production, which is not one of his best, and pours his contempt upon his critical audience: they are "curious fooles, and envious of thy straine", he assures himself, "their pallat's with the Swine". The arrogance is as disturbing as mawkish sentimentality would be, and all the more so because of Jonson's own achieved high standards. Thomas Carew, one of "the tribe of Ben" and a remarkably fine critic, expressed the real weakness of the poem and recognised its betrayal of Jonson's own standards when he wrote, in *To Ben Jonson Upon occasion of his Ode of defiance annext to his play of the new Inne*,

> Why should the follies then of this dull age
> Draw from thy Pen such an immodest rage,
> As seems to blast thy (else immortall) Bayes,
> When thine owne hand proclaims thy ytch of praise?
> Such thirst will argue drought . . .
> The wiser world doth greater Thee confesse
> Than all men else, than Thyself only lesse.

The point is well taken: Jonson's presentation of himself in the Ode does him less than justice. The poem is a sop to his injured pride and the strident note, as the title hints, is of one asserting himself at the expense of his art.

Jonson's works, as Carew reminds us, "are not all alike"; like Shakespeare, he is not always at his best. He is frequently betrayed elsewhere by the arrogance which flaws the *Ode to Himselfe*. On such occasions the limitations of the art and the detachment of the artist are imposed by constrictions of feeling which stem from a profound distaste for the life of the vulgar, something which also expresses itself at times as a feeling for the vulgar tongue. It is this feeling which is at work in the characterisation of Captain Tucca in *Poetaster*, as here in his sense of outrage:

A Player? Call him, call the lowsie slave hither: What will he saile
by, and not once strike, or vaile to a *Man of warre*? ha? do you heare?
you, player, rogue, stalker, come back here: no respect to men of
worship, you slave? What, you are proud, you rascall, are you
proud? ha? you grow rich, doe you? and purchase, you two-penny
tearemouth? you have fortune, and the good yeere on your side,
you stinkard? you have? you have?[15]

Here Jonson's attitude to the *hoi polloi* (like Eliot's in *The Waste Land*)
expresses itself in a mockery of their language; he seems uncomfortable
in his use of that racy colloquialism which came so naturally to his
contemporaries. The captain's language is stiff and stilted; the rhythms
and the repetitions are not those of indignation, they are those of one
who apes offence rather than feels offended.

Jonson's conservatism at times undoubtedly supports an arrogant
sense of superiority to the life he sees about him, even when it is the
life bred in his bones; in *Christmas his Masque* the Londoner "is not
wholly free from a slight tone of patronage towards the customs of the
citizens of London". But whilst his political disposition occasionally
blunts his sympathetic feelings, it sharpens his critical faculties. The
point is nicely made by Mr. Bamborough when he remarks of Jonson
that "His *forte* was the keen observation of human life and the ability to
re-create some aspects of it, not empathy or the ability to enter into the
feelings of others."[16] Our response to this impediment, however,
should be grounded, like Carew's, in a respect for what Jonson so finely
and uniquely represents. The perfect image of his art is one which
recurs in the poems and which places the patronising lapses as those of a
man who, like the farmer in *Praises of a Countrie Life*, cultivates his
native soil:

> The Poplar tall, he then doth marrying twine
>   With the growne issue of the vine;
> And with his hooke lops off the fruitless race,
>   And sets more happy in the place. . . .

The lines not only provide an image of the artist and an ideal of cultivated life, they also express the political attitude (see the conversation
of the gardeners in *Richard II*, III.iv) which informs Jonson's work.
The moral pruning undertaken in the plays, and the marrying and
setting of ideals, performed in the poems and masques, are complementary political activities: the Court and the private reader needed to be
reminded of the old ideals of life; the *hoi polloi* needed to be purged of

the viciousness of the times before those ideals could properly take root and eventually bear fruit. And if we are still disturbed by Jonson's patronising, which also expresses itself in his paternal attitude to his followers, it needs to be remembered that to patronise was for Jonson one of those old ideals, as *To Penshurst* demonstrates. What disturbs is not a failure of art but a limited vision of social life.

Jonson's vision of life was by no means an idiosyncratic one; it had a powerful exponent in Herrick also. The same sense of life informs the poetry of Herrick, who directly addresses the creative principle embodied in the cultivators of the soil:

> Come, sons of summer, by whose toil,
> We are the lords of wine and oil:
> By whose tough labours, and rough hands,
> We rip up first, then reap our lands.[17]

And in Herrick's poetry, too, this creative principle merges into that of art when the "Sons of Summer" are addressed in such lines as:

> Crown'd with the eares of corne, now come,
> And, to the Pipe, sing Harvest home.
> Come forth, my Lord, and see the Cart
> Drest up with all the Country Art.

It is this feeling for the creative principle of rural life which expresses itself as reverence in Herrick, in such a poem as *Corinna's Going a Maying*:

> Come, my *Corinna*, and comming, marke
> How each field turns a street; each a street a Parke
>   Made green, and trimm'd with trees: see how
>   Devotion gives each House a Bough,
>   Or Branch: Each Porch, each doore, ere this,
>   An Arke, a Tabernacle is,
> Made up of white-thorn neatly enterwove;
> As if here were those cooler shades of love.[18]

Here in an act of devotion the homes of "the sons of summer" become arks and tabernacles, containers of the holy spirit. And Jonson's sense of reverence before the household gods, in *To Penshurst* for instance, reflects a devotion for the way of life so succinctly expressed in Herrick's lines. Hence the initial assertion that Jonson's work is inclined and committed to a traditional point of view and a traditional set of values which are more explicitly social, less obviously metaphysical, than those of Donne.

3. THOMAS HOBBES AND THE ART OF POLITICAL THEORY

The art of Donne is that of "a little world made cunningly", a world in which relationships are established by an analogy and dialectic which is a tribute to the intellectual tradition of medieval Europe. Jonson's art is directed by a more intimate concern for the traditional social code, grounded in hospitality, generosity, modesty and simplicity. The art of Thomas Hobbes is neither that of Donne nor that of Jonson; it rejects both the social code and the intellectual tradition. Hobbes dismisses Aristotle and the schoolman with tart humour and looks upon human sociability as the result of fear and narrow self-interest. In consequence his art is prompted by opinions and dispositions which are not only different from those of Donne and Jonson but antagonistic to them, not overtly perhaps but nevertheless fundamentally.

It will no doubt seem strange that the art of Hobbes should be referred to in the same sense as the art of Donne and Jonson. The consensus of enlightened opinion has afforded Hobbes the doubtful reputation of a political theorist, a writer intent primarily upon explaining the institution and the constitution of that great leviathan, the State. His view of the State as an instrument of coercion, which has met with praise from rebels, is grounded in a low opinion of human nature, which has led the same rebels to praise him with faint damns. But his attitude towards human nature would usually be said to have no poetic status, whereas that of Donne and Jonson has no existence apart from their art. But to choose to speak of the art of Hobbes is to draw attention to the fact that the attitudes of Hobbes also belong primarily to the world of art, that they derive from fiction and masquerade as speculation.

That Hobbes is concerned for art is evident enough in *The Answer to the Preface to Gondibert* and in many passages in *Leviathan*, but the art which constitutes the framework of Hobbes' vision of the world, and of the political world in particular, is best indicated in the Introduction to *Leviathan*:

> Nature, the art whereby God hath made and governs the world, is by the art of man, as in many other things, so in this also imitated, that it can make an artificial animal. For seeing life is but a motion of limbs, the beginning whereof is in some principal part within; why may we not say, that all automata (engines that move themselves by springs and wheels as doth a watch) have an artificial life? For what is the heart, but a spring; and the nerves, but so many

strings; and the joints, but so many wheels, giving motion to the whole body, such as was intended by the artificer? Art goes yet further, imitating that rational and most excellent work of nature, man. For by art is created that great Leviathan called a Commonwealth, or State, in Latin Civitas, which is but an artificial man; though of greater stature and strength than the natural, for whose protection and defence it was intended; and in which the sovereignty is an artificial soul, as giving life and motion to the whole body; the magistrates, and other officers of judicature and execution, artificial joints; reward and punishment, by which fastened to the seat of the sovereignty every joint and member is moved to perform his duty, are the nerves, that do the same in the body natural; the wealth and riches of all the particular members, are the strength; *salus populi*, the people's safety, its business; counsellors, by whom all things needful for it to know are suggested unto it, are the memory; equity, and laws, an artificial reason and will; concord, health; sedition, sickness; and civil war, death. Lastly, the pacts and covenants, by which the parts of this body politic were at first made, set together, and united, resemble that *fiat*, or the *let us make man*, pronounced by God in the creation.[1]

Here Hobbes' attitude towards art is essentially the same as that which we meet with in Pope, for like Pope he accepts the traditional view that the world is a work of art created by God. On this view the highest, or as Pope would say, the true form of art is "Nature, the art whereby God hath made and governs the world," whilst the art of man, God's most excellent artifice, is merely an imitation of Nature, the true and divine art. It is, therefore, by *art*, by imitating Nature, that man contrives both his technology (or automata, to use Hobbes' term) and that complex instrument of government "called a Commonwealth, or State".

Hobbes, of course, is using the word *art* in its older and to my mind its best sense to mean creation; it is in this sense that Jonson refers to his son as "Ben. Ionson his best piece of poetrie". Human art is a skill and all skills are governed by the imagination, which, as Hobbes explains later, may be either simple, "which is the imagining the whole object as it was presented to the sense", or compound, as when images of a man and a horse are compounded to produce the image of a centaur, which Hobbes describes as "a fiction of the mind". It follows that for Hobbes art is intent both upon seeing things as they really are and upon inventing things which never were. His doctrine of the imagination is therefore similar to that of Wordsworth and Coleridge, who distin-

guish between the primary imagination and the fancy, or secondary
imagination, along lines similar to Hobbes.

On the traditional view which Hobbes adopts, therefore, *Leviathan*
is a work of art and it is with this in mind that the reference to the art
of Hobbes has to be understood. This does not displace the contention
that Hobbes is a political theorist, it simply suggests that a more precise
formulation would be that the art of Hobbes is directed towards the
creation of a political theory. Put thus precisely, one can appreciate
that *Leviathan* is an imaginative work, in Hobbes' sense of imagination,
and that in order to appraise it correctly, therefore, one needs to know
what order of imagination is involved: is it that simple imagination,
which sees things as they really are, or is it that compound imagination,
which is "a fiction of the mind"?

The art with which Hobbes opens his case, in the passage already
quoted at length, is one familiar to us from our reading of Donne, it is
the art of analogy or of arguing poetically by simile and metaphor.
In the quoted passage it begins with an axiom, "life is but a motion of
limbs, the beginning whereof is in some principal part within", and
proceeds to the analogy between a piece of machinery and the body of
an animal in order to establish that man is capable by art of producing
"an artificial life". Hobbes then proceeds to an analogy between the
body of man and the organs of State in order to establish that the State
is a gigantic man, the life of which is similarly produced by art and
which is therefore an "artificial man". Now there is no question but
that this is an imaginative conception and that it consists not in seeing
things as they really are but in compounding different things so as to
produce "a fiction of the mind", which is the Leviathan or State.

Hobbes' *Leviathan*, then, sets out as a work of the compound imagination or fancy. It is essentially a work of wit, in the sense in which
Donne's poetry is said to be witty, rather than a work of judgment,
such as we might expect from a political theorist. Once again, this
placing of Hobbes may appear strange to a philosopher and yet it is
the one most consistent with the views expounded by Hobbes. In
Chapter VIII of *Leviathan*, "Of the Virtues Commonly Called Intellectual; and Their Contrary Defects", he himself defines good wit and
distinguishes it from good judgment, along much the same lines as does
Pope in *Essay on Criticism*. Good wit, he remarks, consists of quickness
of imagination, which

is caused by the difference of men's passions: that love and dislike,
some one thing, some another: and therefore some men's thoughts

run one way, some another; and are held to, and observe differently the things that pass through their imagination. And whereas in this succession of men's thoughts, there is nothing to observe in the things they think on, but either in what they be like one another, or in what they be unlike, or what they serve for, or how they serve to such a purpose; those that observe their similitudes, in case they be such as are but rarely observed by others, are said to have a good wit; by which, in this occasion, is meant a good fancy. . . . But they that observe their differences, and dissimilitudes; which is called distinguishing, and discerning, and judging between thing and thing; in case such discerning be not easy, are said to have a good judgment. . . . The former, that is, fancy, without the help of judgment, is not commended as a virtue; but the latter which is judgment, and discretion, is commended for itself, without the help of fancy.[2]

It is, then, not by good judgment—i.e. by distinguishing between life and mechanical operation, man and the state—but by good wit, i.e. by assimilating different things, that Hobbes arrives at the conception of Leviathan. This, in itself, does not vitiate the argument which Hobbes advances, and he explicitly recognises that such assimilation may be useful in explaining a philosophic point of view. What does vitiate the argument is his insistence upon the fundamental distinction between partial assimilation, or similitude, and complete assimilation, or metaphor.

In demonstration, in counsel, and all rigorous search of truth, the judgment does all, except sometimes the understanding have need to be opened by some apt similitude; and then there is so much use of fancy. But for metaphors, they are in this case utterly excluded. For seeing they openly profess deceit; to admit them into counsel, or reasoning, were manifest folly.[3]

The grounds of this distinction are traditional: metaphors are deceits because they represent one thing as some different thing—a simile claims, for example, that a man is *like* a monkey, a metaphor that a man *is* a monkey; for some purposes the one may be a useful comparison, the other is invariably a falsehood.*

It is evident, therefore, that Hobbes' conception of Leviathan, which

---

* A falsehood, not a lie, because a metaphor, although used to persuade, is not necessarily intended to deceive. A metaphor may represent something in a false light, but the falsity may be due to a mistaken notion on the part of the user and may not therefore be an intentional deception.

proceeds from such assertions as "For what is the heart, but a spring; and the nerves, but so many strings; and the joints but so many wheels," is arrived at by metaphor, or poetic reasoning, and not by judgment and a "rigorous search of truth" assisted by similitudes. Therefore, whilst the art of Hobbes does elsewhere depend upon the use of judgment, the central and organising image of *Leviathan* is a poetic one, "a fiction of the mind" produced by the operation of the wit and fancy.

The image of the state which represents it as the body of a man is a traditional one. Thomas Starkey is explaining a commonplace when he describes the body politic in his *Dialogue Between Pole and Lupset,* written in the 1530's:

> For this body hath his parts, which resemble also the parts of the body of man, of which the most general to our purpose be these: the heart, head, hands and feet. The heart thereof is the king, prince and ruler of the state, whethersoever it be one or many, according to the governance of the commonalty and politic state. . . . He or they which have authority upon the whole state right well may be resembled to the heart. For like as all wit, reason and sense, feeling, life and all other natural power springeth out of the heart, so from the princes and rulers of the state cometh all laws, order and policy, all justice, virtue and honesty, to the rest of this politic body. To the head, with the eyes, ears and other senses therein, resembled may be right well the under-officers by princes appointed, forasmuch as they should ever observe and diligently wait for the weal of the rest of this body. To the hands are resembled both craftsmen and warriors which defend the rest of the body from injury of enemies outward, and work and make things necessary to the same. To the feet, the ploughmen and tillers of the ground, because they by their labour sustain and support the rest of the body. These are the most general parts of this politic body, which may justly be resembled, after the manner declared, to those chief parts in man's body.

And Starkey concludes,

> Now, as I said, the strength of these parts altogidder is of necessity required, without the which the health of the whole cannot long be maintained.[4]

The same image is used by Shakespeare in the opening of *Coriolanus* and is used to make the same point, namely that social life is homogeneous, the point which Donne is making when he declares that "no man is an island, entire of itself; every man is a piece of the continent, a part of the main; if a clod be washed away by the sea, Europe is the less, as well as if a promotory were, as well as if a manor of thy friends or of thine own were: any man's death diminishes me, because I am involved in mankind".[5] This is the traditional use of the image of the state or commonweal as the body of a man, to illustrate the sense in which each member of society is involved in society as a whole.*

Hobbes' image of society, however, is fundamentally different from the traditional one we meet with in Starkey, Shakespeare and Donne. For the traditional image expresses a belief in sociability as a basic fact of human nature. The *Leviathan* of Hobbes, on the other hand, represents human alienation and expresses a belief that men are naturally antagonistic individuals, whose natural state of existence is one of a war "of every man against every man", in which condition

> there is no place for industry; because the fruit thereof is uncertain: and consequently no culture of the earth; no navigation, nor use of the commodities that may be imported by sea; no commodious building; no instrument of moving, and removing, such things as require much force; no knowledge of the face of the earth; no account of time; no arts; no letters; no society; and which is worst of all, continual fear, and danger of violent death; and the life of man, solitary, poor, nasty, brutish and short.[6]

This may well be a fair enough description of primitive man's condition,† but it is one which results from the very limited technology of primitive man and not from man's natural antagonism to man. Indeed, there is more reason to suppose that man is naturally gregarious, a herd animal rather than a maverick, and that in this respect the traditional view is essentially correct.

There is much to be said in favour of Hobbes' view of human history: he is aware that man is of primitive rather than prelapsarian origin, that is to say, that he has risen rather than fallen, and this is an opinion he arrives at empirically, or at least one he supports on empirical grounds, by referring to what he calls "American savages", by which he must mean the Indians since he was writing before Chicago had policemen. What one questions, however, is not what Hobbes believes to be the facts of human history, but the attitude which he adopts

---

* Donne makes an explicit and detailed use of the image in "Meditation 17" (*Devotions Upon Emergent Occasions*, pp. 69–70).

† This is a concession for the sake of argument. Primitive man has to be industrious to scratch together a bare subsistence. His life was certainly not solitary nor as short and poor as that of a miner or mill-worker of the last century

towards human nature and human existence. On the Hobbesian view human nature alternates between that of a cornered rat and that of a mad dog, a natural human existence is one of permanent and vicious competition. Man is by nature, it seems, bloody-minded and piratical, intent either upon guarding his loot or upon acquiring it by rapine and murder.

It is in this respect that the art of Hobbes is peculiarly modern, as that of Donne and Jonson is not. For whilst the art of Donne and Jonson proceeds from a vision of a tightly integrated human community, that of Hobbes plainly proceeds from a vision of a society of violently competing individuals whose acquisitiveness has to be restrained by a powerful State apparatus. In other and blunter words, the art of Hobbes is that of a capitalist society and he is perhaps the first writer to equate society, or what he calls civil society, with capitalist society. For Hobbes, the existence of a powerful State machine, or *Leviathan*, is definitive of civil society; historically, it is definitive of a capitalist society: in England such a machine does not emerge until the sixteenth century and the rise of capitalism. For Hobbes, the State machine was needed to constrain human acquisitiveness, to prevent men despoiling their neighbours; historically, it legalised acquisitive behaviour, which had previously been prohibited, and encouraged the expansion of trade at the expense of local self-sufficiency by providing commerce with safe facilities. Far from restraining those who coveted their neighbour's ox and ass, the State ensured the repeal of the ban on usury, supported those who acted against the traditional edicts of the just price and the just wage, made acquisition a respectable motive in life and provided opportunities for rapacity on a scale previously unknown. In short, far from Hobbes' Leviathan superseding a world of competing individuals in which either you or your neighbour went to the wall, it was directly responsible for instituting such a state of affairs and establishing it as a normal condition of English social life.

It is this new condition of life that is realised in the art of Hobbes and it is this which makes it so peculiarly modern. Just as his Leviathan represents the rejection of the old local and patriarchal rights and duties of feudalism, so his intellectual position is a rejection of the doctrines and points of view which constituted the ideological foundation of the traditional arrangements of social life. His sceptical view of the old philosophy, whatever its merits, is a deliberate devaluation of the intellectual tradition and an attack not simply upon ideas but upon institutions, upon the "tenets of vain philosophy, derived to the

Universities,* and thence into the Church, partly from Aristotle, partly from the blindness of understanding".[7] It was the Church, of course, which was responsible for propagating traditional social doctrine and Hobbes' attack upon Aristotle and the schoolmen is, in effect, an attack upon the social doctrines of the Church and therefore an essential part of his general onslaught upon traditional attitudes towards the organisation of social life.

The art of Hobbes is as much an art of living as that of Ben Jonson and, like Jonson's, it is normative, but the norms projected with powerful realism are those of a society quite unlike that informing Jonson's art. For Jonson, as for Shakespeare, respect, friendship and hospitality are basic needs of human nature sanctioned by the natural order of things and not, as Hobbes represents them, merely part of the sophisticated veneer of civilised man, imposed by fear and the sword. Despite the real power of Hobbes' art, it remains a black art, undermining man's self-respect and preparing the mind to acquiesce in the brutalities of the new society on the grounds that such brutalities are simple facts of human nature.

* Those who nowadays are intent upon defending the traditions of the Universities need to be reminded that those traditions would not have been established if those who were defending the traditions of the Universities in Hobbes' day had succeeded.

4

Crisis and Resolution

*Though there were many clever men in England during the latter half of
the seventeenth century there were only two minds which possessed the
imaginative faculty in a very eminent degree. One of those minds produced
the Paradise Lost, the other the Pilgrim's Progress.*

Macaulay[1]

I. 'PARADISE LOST' AND THE PURITAN DEBACLE

Milton, although composed of only six letters, is a big name, or to put
the matter more precisely, a big reputation. It is not too difficult to
formulate the various contentions upon which this reputation rests.
Many of these can be attended to by considering Milton's "grand
manner". As I understand it, the following passage from the first book
of *Paradise Lost* is a not too unusual illustration of the "grand manner".
Satan has been flung down beside Beelzebub:

> To whom th' Arch-Enemy,
> And thence in Heav'n calld Satan, with bold words
> Breaking the horrid silence thus began.
>   If thou beest he; But o how fall'n! how chang'd
> From him, who in the happy Realms of Light,
> Cloth'd with transcendent brightness didst outshine
> Myriads though bright: If he whom mutual league,
> United thoughts and counsels, equal hope
> And hazard in the Glorious Enterprize,
> Joined with me once, now misery hath joind
> In equal ruin: into what Pit thou seest
> From what highth fall'n, so much the stronger prov'd
> Hee with his Thunder: and till then who knew
> The force of those dire Arms?[2]

Where, to begin with, is the famous organ music, that highly commended roll of sonorous sound? The blundering rhythms of the
passage grope about as though in search of some elusive thought:

H

> If thou beest he; But o how fall'n! how chang'd
> From him, who in the happy Realms of Light,
> Cloth'd with transcendent brightness didst outshine
> Myriads, though bright . . .

The ramshackle movement of the lines is determined by the shoddy syntax. Furthermore, the grammar of Satan's sentence is so atrocious that one is tempted to believe he has been sent down because his English was likely to bring Heaven into disrepute.

Despite its weaknesses and confusions, *Paradise Lost* has provided innumerable readers with a sense of its own lively importance. In part this is due to the poetic aura of the work: after all, it is an epic, it deals with a fundamental Christian theme and it does so in a manner assuming greatness from the outset, when the poet calls upon the heavenly Muse,

> That to the highth of this great Argument
> I may assert Eternal Providence,
> And Justifie the wayes of God to men. [3]

The tone and vocabulary are portentous and the poem continuously reminds us of the immensity of its theme: description is constantly unfocussed by such adjectives as 'perpetual', 'eternal', 'transcendent', 'omnipotent'. The imagination is continually stone-walled by the unimaginable and, in its place, a sense of awe emerges. Everything in the poem tends to the sustenance of this awesomeness, which becomes the primary product of the "grand manner" and an essential part of the matter of the poem. The famous "organ music", when it comes into play, operates by carrying the eye forward compulsively from clause to clause, offering this 'ear' a rhythmical substitute for syntax and hence for sense. It is the procedure of diverting the attention by an accumulation of clauses and carrying it forward by sonorous rhythms that induces the reader to accept the portentousness of the poem at face value.

One might say of the style of *Paradise Lost*, therefore, that it is filled with a sense of its own importance. And bearing in mind Aristotle's dictum, the style is the man, the implications of this are unavoidable. From a tender age Milton believed himself to be elect of the Muses and dedicated himself to preparation for some great poetic work; a dedication and a sense of election which later became subtly entwined with Puritan doctrine. The two are blended in *Paradise Lost*, when in the opening of Book VIII the poet calls upon Urania,

> still govern thou my Song,
> Urania, and fit audience find, though few.[4]

The elect of the Muses, therefore, addresses himself to a small band, the Puritan elect, whose fitness is well defined for us by Abdiel when he opposes Satan with,

> my Sect thou seest, now learn too late
> How few sometimes may know, when thousands err.[5]

The doctrine plainly lends itself to the feeling of self-importance which characterises the man in the style of *Paradise Lost*. It is not at all surprising, therefore, that we should encounter passages in the poem in which Milton appears to be involved in surreptitious self-appraisal. To the last two passages quoted might be added that towards the beginning of Book VI in which God declares,

> Servant of God, well done, well hast thou fought
> The better fight, who single hast maintain'd
> Against revolted multitudes the Cause
> Of Truth, in word mightier than they in Armes;
> And for the testimonie of Truth has born
> Universal reproach, far worse to beare
> Then violence; for this was all thy care
> To stand approv'd in sight of God, though Worlds
> Judg'd thee perverse.[6]

Here we are in the presence of Milton himself, isolated and outcast after the Restoration and yet still strong in the beliefs to which he had dedicated his life.* It is something of this strength which carries one through *Paradise Lost* and it is to this I shall return later.

Milton's slighter poems rank more highly as achievements than *Paradise Lost*; in attempting less they naturally improved their chances of success. However, even in these poems there are discrepancies between what is offered and what is achieved, as may be seen in *Lycidas*. What initially the poem offers is stated in the opening lines:

> Yet once more, O ye Laurels, and once more
> Ye Myrtles brown, with Ivy never-sear,
> I com to pluck your Berries harsh and crude,
> And with forc'd fingers rude,
> Shatter your leaves before the mellowing year.
> Bitter constraint, and sad occasion dear,
> Compels me to disturb your season due:

---

* A somewhat similar situation is realised in that of Samson in *Samson Agonistes*.

> For Lycidas is dead, dead ere his prime
> Young Lycidas, and hath not left his peer.[7]

The offer to disturb the equanimity of nature is what gives vigour to the opening lines and informs the diction—*harsh, crude, forc'd, Shatter, Bitter constraint, Compels*. The compulsive energy is felt as it defines the response to the death of Lycidas in terms of a violent act against nature. The poem, however, shifts into a reminiscent mood in the lines which follow and assumes that air of day-dream which establishes its relation to Spenser. It then returns to the present but retains the mood of reverie:

> But O the heavy change, now thou art gon,
> Now thou art gon, and never must return!
> Thee Shepherd, thee the Woods, and desert Caves,
> With wild Thyme and the gadding vine o'ergrown,
> And all their echoes mourn.
> The Willows, and the Hazel copses green,
> Shall now no more be seen,
> Fanning their joyous Leaves to thy soft layes.
> As killing as the Canker to the Rose,
> Or Taint-worm to the weanling Herds that graze,
> Or Frost to Flowers, that their gay wardrobe wear,
> When first the White-thorn blows;
> Such, Lycidas, thy loss to Shepherds ear.[8]

The early vigour is here replaced by a sense of ease and relaxation and the poem gently meanders. It may be urged that the poem has moved from the violence of fresh grief to that calmer appraisal of death which time and reflection naturally accomplishes and that this transition is perfectly acceptable. However, it is not the transition that is disconcerting, but the quality of the calmer appraisal. The initial response to the death of Lycidas as a violation of nature places an implicit value upon death. Later this evaluation changes, a consequence no doubt of calmer reflection, and we see the death of Lycidas as a particular kind of natural event,

> As killing as the Canker to the Rose,
> Or Taint-worm to the weanling Herds that graze,
> Or Frost to Flowers, that their gay wardrobe wear,
> When first the White-thorn blows. . . .

The appraisal of naturalness has subtly changed in order, as it were, to accommodate, to soften and beautify the fact of death. Death now finds its place in a nature which is gently idyllic. In brief, calmer reflection does not lead to a more precise concentration upon the event but to remoteness from it; it softens death by softening and prettifying nature.*

Just as the compulsive vigour of the opening lines defines the initial response to the death of Lycidas, so does the air of gentle fantasy define the concern for fame to which the poem now proceeds:

> Alas! What boots it with uncessant care
> To tend the homely slighted Shepherds trade,
> And strictly meditate the thankless Muse,
> Were it not better don as others use,
> To sport with Amaryllis in the shade,
> Or with the tangles of Neaera's hair?
> Fame is the spur that the clear spirit doth raise
> (That last infirmity of Noble mind)
> To scorn delights, and live laborious dayes;
> But the fair Guerdon when we hope to find,
> And think to burst out into sudden blaze,
> Comes the blind Fury with th' abhorred shears,
> And slits the thin-spun life. But not the praise,
> Phoebus repli'd, and touch'd my trembling ears;
> Fame is no plant that grows on mortal soil,
> Nor in the glistering foil
> Set off to th' world, nor in broad rumour lies,
> But lives and spreds aloft by those pure eyes,
> And perfect witnes of all-judging Jove;
> As he pronounces lastly on each deed,
> Of so much fame in Heav'n expect thy meed.[9]

Once again, as in *Paradise Lost*, the personality of Milton is subtly involved in the poetry. The passage moves from the distinguishable idyllic fantasy of the homely, slighted shepherd and those who

> sport with Amaryllis in the shade,
> Or with the tangles of Neaera's hair,

to the explanation of the shepherd's motives:

> Fame is the spur that the clear spirit doth raise
> (That last infirmity of Noble mind)
> To scorn delights, and live laborious dayes. . . .

Behind that explanatory justification one senses the pressure of Milton's own aspirations to poetic fame. Yet the passage itself has firmly placed

---

* Here again the connection with Spenser makes itself felt (see p. 40–1 above).

the justification, and hence Milton's aspiration, in a world of idyllic fantasy. The aspiration sensed is as remote from reality as the pastoral shepherd, Amaryllis and Neaera. And it is precisely here, where Milton becomes personally involved, that we note the confusion which, on a larger scale, characterises *Paradise Lost*. The relevant lines are

> Fame is the spur that the clear spirit doth raise
> (That last infirmity of Noble mind). . . .

Presumably we are intended to straighten out the syntax for ourselves and to understand the sense of the lines as "Fame, that last infirmity of noble mine, is the spur that the clear spirit doth raise". But, although this is how many readers understand the lines, this is not what they actually say; "that last infirmity of noble mind", according to the lines of the poem, is not Fame but "the clear spirit". What is involved is an unwitting truth about Milton's own fame, for it is the "last infirmity", clarity, which is overcome in achieving the full nobility of mind expressed in *Paradise Lost*.

   Lycidas, however, does have some bearing upon the real abilities of Milton. It is a pastoral poem, concerning a shepherd; but 'pastoral' also suggests 'of the pastor' and the shepherd brings to mind the Christian pastor. This analogy informs the poem and it is the concern for the state of contemporary pastors that re-invigorates it. The promise of the opening lines is made good in such lines as:

> How well could I have spar'd for thee young swain,
> Anow of such as for their bellies sake,
> Creep and intrude, and climb into the fold?
> Of other care they little reck'ning make,
> Then how to scramble at the shearers feast,
> And shove away the worthy bidden guest;
> Blind mouthes! that scarce themselves know how to hold
> A Sheep-hook, or have learn'd ought els the least
> That to the faithful Herdmans art belongs!
> What recks it them? What need they? They are sped;
> And when they list, their lean and flashy songs
> Grate on their scrannel Pipes of wretched straw,
> The hungry Sheep look up, and are not fed,
> But swoln with wind, and the rank mist they draw,
> Rot inwardly, and foul contagion spread:
> Besides what the grim Woolf with privy paw
> Daily devours apace, and nothing sed.[10]

Indignation builds up in the passage as the false shepherds grow bolder and finds its expression in a racy language which gives physical presence to their nastiness; they *creep, scramble, shove*, are *lean, flashy, rank*. It is not so much the indignation that gives the passage its power as the idiomatic bite of the language. Here Milton's language suddenly achieves an Englishness which is intimately expressive of the life of rural England and consequently appropriate to the pastoralism of the poem.

As in the opening lines of *Lycidas*, then, it is once again indignation that determines the quality of the language. It is as though the surge of protest placed the poet in contact with his native tongue and so with native English life. It is this rebellious element in Milton's style, in *Lycidas, Comus* and *Paradise Lost*, that from time to time brushes aside the inclination to fantasy and egoism. Milton's real strength lay here and in the connections with contemporary life which this suggests rather than in his aspirations to epic grandeur.

Milton's long preparation for a great epic attempt is well known; so too is his eventual rejection of a scheme to found his epic upon the romance of King Arthur and his knights and his decision to take as his subject the Revolt and Fall of the Angels and the Fall of Man. The story was familiar and in this respect at least *Paradise Lost* does not pursue "Things unattempted yet in Prose or Rhime". Neither can one believe, considering the immense body of Christian apologetic that had accumulated over the centuries, that there was anything new in Milton's hope,

> That to the highth of this great Argument
> I may assert Eternal Providence,
> And justifie the wayes of God to men.

If that hope had the colour of newness it was borrowed from the historical circumstances in which Milton produced the poem rather than from the general nature of the task itself. There was, that is to say, a particular historical need to justify the ways of God to men and to assert Eternal Providence and that need was the collapse and the eventual overthrow of the Puritan Reformation, the failure to build Jerusalem in England's green and pleasant land. I am by no means suggesting that any such need was present to Milton's mind, but only that the circumstances of the times created in the Puritan consciousness a new preoccupation with the way of God towards men. That God had once again apparently forsaken his chosen people must have been a thought that sent the Puritan remnant groping for explanations, blindly seeking to exonerate the Lord, searching their own actions for the sin which enabled Satan to enter and lay waste the New Jerusalem.

It is, I believe, in terms of this bewilderment that one can best appreciate Milton's style and see most clearly its connection both with the circumstances of the times and the task Milton set himself in *Paradise Lost*. In short, *Paradise Lost* realises the basic preoccupations, and the state of mind in which these were pursued, not of one lonely individual, but of a multitude of men and women. The style of the poem, as well as the matter, is that shaped by a Puritan in the collapse of his hopes and his sense of defeat at the hands of God.

Milton's faith, like that of the multitude of Puritans, remains unshaken; in evidence of which we have the immense confidence of *Paradise Lost*, that confidence immediately present in the hope

> That to the highth of this great Argument
> I may assert Eternal Providence
> And justifie the wayes of God to men.

It is a confidence more generally present in the sonorousness of the "grand manner". But working within this large assurance are those peculiarities of style mentioned at the outset, which may be further illustrated from the early part of Book VIII:

> When I behold this goodly Frame, this World
> Of Heav'n and Earth consisting, and compute
> Thir magnitudes, this Earth a spot, a graine,
> An Atom, with the Firmanent compar'd
> And all her numbered Starrs, that seem to rowle
> Spaces incomprehensible (for such
> Thir distance argues and their swift return
> Diurnal) meerly to officiat light
> Round this opacous Earth, this punctual spot,
> One day and night; in all their vast survey
> Useless besides; reasoning I oft admire,
> How Nature wise and frugal could commit
> Such disproportions, with superfluous hand
> So many nobler Bodies to create,
> Greater so manifold, to this one use,
> For aught appeers, and on thir Orbs impose
> Such restless revolution day by day
> Repeated, while the sedentarie Earth,
> That better might with farr less compass move,

> Serv'd by more noble than her self, attaines
> Her end without least motion, and receaves
> As Tribute such a sumless journey brought
> Of incorporeal speed, her warmth and light;
> Speed, to describe whose swiftness Number failes.[11]

This is Adam, following his declaration to Raphael that "something yet of doubt remaines" with a sentence that stumbles about amongst a maze of observations and qualifications, seeking to express his perplexity. The sense of a man searching for what it is that is troubling him, seeking to put his finger upon a nagging but elusive worry, renders itself in slight particulars also; in that attempt to concentrate the attention upon the insignificance of the Earth, "a spot, a graine, An Atom".

This perplexity, created by the actual quality of Milton's writing, at this point defines Adam as a character perplexed by a doubt which he has difficulty in formulating with precision. But the fineness of the passage, the fineness with which Milton realises this perplexity, is due to Milton's own perplexities; he is realising his own predominant state of mind and, indeed, that state of mind which one presumes to have been predominant amongst the faithful Puritans at the apparently inexplicable withdrawal of God's grace from their cause.

That what in this passage is a relevant perplexity is a quality of Milton's style, and one which often leads to confusion, may be judged by referring back to that passage, quoted at the outset, in which Satan addresses Beelzebub in Book I. It is possible, I suppose, although the possibility here is weaker, to argue that this confusion is also relevant, since it serves to realise the confusion of the defeated Satan. One could again urge that this relevance is due to that sense of defeat at the hands of God which Satan here shares with the Puritans. Doubtless some such case could be made out for the majority of examples one would wish to quote in order to illustrate the confusion and perplexity of Milton. But this must lead one on, then, to urge that confusion and perplexity are of the very substance of *Paradise Lost*.

The doubt that Adam broaches to Raphael develops into an inquisition upon astronomy: is the Earth the centre of the universe or is it not? The Ptolemaic and Copernican hypotheses are carefully weighed, but Raphael will commit himself to neither. The conclusion as to

> Whether the Sun predominant in Heav'n
> Rise on the Earth, or Earth rise on the Sun . . .

is

> Solicit not thy thoughts with matters hid
> Leave them to God above, him serve and feare.[12]

Strange doctrine this when one recalls that Milton was a friend of Galileo. Stranger still when, in Book IX, Satan, who should know, appears to accept without question the old Ptolemaic, geocentric theory, praising Earth as

> Terrestrial Heav'n, danc't round by other Heav'ns
> That shine, yet bear thir bright officious Lamps,
> Light above light, for thee alone, as seems,
> In thee concentring all thir precious beams
> Of sacred influence: As God in Heav'n
> Is Center, yet extends to all, so thou
> Centring receav'st from all those Orbs . . .[13]

But why the discussion of astronomy at the beginning of Book VIII anyway?

The doubt and the discussion which follows serves to establish something of the intellectual freedom enjoyed by Adam, freedom to speculate upon the propriety of God's creation, an independence which manifests itself again a little later when we are told of Adam's argument with God concerning Adam's need for a female companion. Consequently, when he agrees with Raphael's command,

> Solicit not thy thoughts with matters hid,
> Leave them to God above . . . ,

it has been established that Adam's agreement concerns what man should not and not what he cannot do. In brief, the discussion offers us an illustration of the willing submission of man's intellect to God. But it seems to point to something more than this. The doubt which Adam initially expressed gives rise to a discussion which ends inconclusively with Raphael's command, and yet Adam declares himself satisfied:

> How fully hast thou satisfi'd me, pure
> Intelligence of Heav'n, Angel serene,
> And freed from intricacies, taught to live
> The easiest way, nor with perplexing thoughts
> To interrupt the sweet of Life, from which
> God hath bid dwell farr off all anxious cares,
> And not molest us, unless wee our selves
> Seek them with wandring thoughts, and notions vain.[14]

The discussion, then, is also an illustration of *doubt, intricacies, perplexing thoughts, anxious cares, wandring thoughts*. What is offered in the conclusion is a suggestion as to how these may be stilled and overcome: *Leave them to God above*.

Here, then, with the doubts, intricacies and anxieties of a mind pondering upon the ways of God, groping to understand the ways of Providence, we are once again exposed to the psychology of the Puritan debacle and the questions which must have possessed the minds of the Elect at the blasting of their hopes. The advice offered, however, reflects the quietism that was invading the Puritan ranks at the time; the feeling that if man had failed to bring the millennium, God would doubtless do so in his own good time. This new spirit can extend, as in *Paradise Lost*, beyond the sphere of practical action into the realms of knowledge. Richard Baxter, a contemporary of Milton, provides a comment upon this aspect of the discussion between Raphael and Adam. In his *Dying Thoughts* Baxter asks,

> If an angel from heaven came down on earth to tell us all of God that we would know, who would not turn his back on libraries and universities, to go and discourse with such a messenger?[15]

The knowledge of God to be gained from such a messenger, Baxter continues,

> will have no mixture of dark and bewildered uncertainty and ambiguity, when it is acquired. It will be perfectly free from those contentions, which so much rob the ingenious of their time, destroy their love, hinder their minds from ascending to God and heavenly things.[16]

And just as Raphael satisfied Adam by bidding him not to bother his head with perplexing problems but leave them to God above, so Baxter suggests that man should wait until he gets to Heaven, for "All those strange and difficult things . . . will then be plain".

We have, then, in Milton the same quietistic confidence that is illustrated by Baxter, resolving doubts by leaving them to Heaven. But Milton also expresses the anxieties and perplexities of a mind groping in bewildered uncertainty. This incongruity between the confidence and the perplexity of *Paradise Lost* is of the very substance of the poem. It is definitive of Milton's art, a fact recognised by Macaulay where he referred to

The peculiar art which [Milton] possessed of communicating his meaning circuitously through a long succession of associated ideas, and of intimating more than he expressed,

an art which, Macaulay concluded, "enabled him to disguise those incongruities which he could not avoid".[17] That the incongruities are there in *Paradise Lost* is generally admitted; it is also evident that they are disguised to some extent by Milton's style, "communicating his meaning circuitously through a long succession of associated ideas", what I would describe as a perplexed groping after some satisfactory conclusion. That the discussion between Raphael and Adam, for example, reaches a satisfactory conclusion is doubtful; if one is satisfied with it, this is because one is discouraged by the very circuitous nature of the expression from paying serious attention to it. And to arrive at a general observation from this particular one, it appears that the satisfaction given to the reader, like that given by Raphael to Adam, relies upon the absence of serious attention to the matter in hand. In still more general terms, the confidence of Milton, that pervading confidence that sounds in the sonorousness of his language and the forward sweep of his rhythms and procures some satisfaction, is supported by no particular seriousness of the intellect. The incongruity between these two elements of Milton's style is analogous to that between faith and reason. The movement of the poetry has an assurance that derives from faith, faith in the conclusion towards which it moves with such confidence; the fumbling logic, the lack of particular grip upon the argument, derives from a failure to support that large faith with reason. Indeed, Milton's quietistic doctrine of knowledge represents this failure as a test of faith.

Such peculiarities of style need to be appraised in the context of that crisis of Puritan consciousness which followed the 'failure' of the Puritan Reformation. It is not difficult to appreciate that for a Puritan in such circumstances this failure pointed to some inherent weakness in human nature, to man's liability to err, or sin, as he would more forthrightly have called it.

The first, more or less explicit, suggestion that Milton's own predicament is being realised in the characterisation of Adam occurs towards the end of Book VIII, when Adam is attempting to explain to Raphael his feelings towards Eve. Nature, Adam observes, has bestowed on Eve

> Too much of Ornament, in outward shew
> Elaborate, of inward less exact.[18]

He continues by drawing a distinction between the beauty of her outward form and her inferiority "in the mind and inward Faculties". In many respects this characterisation of Eve is also a characterisation of Milton's own poetry—outwardly attractive, inwardly less exact. I am not suggesting that Milton is deliberately appraising himself, simply that in the creation of Eve Milton reveals the same predicament as that revealed in the poetry at large. Despite Eve's lack of inward exactness, Adam observes,

> when I approach
> Her loveliness, so absolute she seems
> And in herself compleat, so well to know
> Her own, that what she wills to do or say,
> Seems wisest, vertuousest, discreetest, best;
> All higher knowledge in her presence falls
> Degraded . . .[19]

One is immediately reminded of those numerous appraisals of Milton's poetry which insist that we should attend to its architectonic qualities, its overall majesty—so absolute, so complete, that whatever it does "Seems wisest, vertuousest, discreetest, best"—in other words, that appreciation of Milton that argues that we approach him wrongly in being too particular. To argue thus is to follow Adam and fall into the trap laid by that word *Seems*. True, if we allow ourselves to be captured by the apparent grandeur of the poetry we never question its inward exactness and what it does "*Seems* wisest, vertuousest . . ." Just as, if Adam allows himself to be captured by the apparent grandeur and beauty of Eve, then he too is carried into believing that what she does "*Seems* wisest . . ." But Raphael is there to remind us and Adam that it is not a question of what *seems* wisest and best, but of what *is* wisest and best—

> For what admir'st thou, what transports thee so;
> An outside? Fair no doubt, and worthy well
> Thy cherishing, thy honouring, and thy love,
> Not thy subjection . . .[20]

It is a reprimand one wishes to give those who have urged us to surrender, or subject, ourselves to the architectonic of Milton. Whilst admitting that Milton's 'organ music' carries us along in a cloud of feeling or passion one needs also to remember Raphael's warning to Adam—

> take heed least Passion sway
> Thy Judgement . . .[21]

The connection between Adam and Milton is fairly obvious. If Adam surrenders reason to passion, he allegorises Milton's own condition, in which the reason or logic of the language is sacrificed to the passions or feelings expressed in the rhythms of the language. There is, however, a major distinction between the assurance and dedication of Adam in these passages and that assurance and dedication which finds expression in the movement of Milton's poetry. To put it crudely, Milton's assurance is an assurance in God and in his attempt "to justifie the wayes of God to men"; Adam's is an assurance in Eve and a dedication to her that is epitomised in his observation,

> I now see
> Bone of my Bone, Flesh of my Flesh, my Self
> Before me; Woman is her Name, of Man
> Extracted; for this cause he shall forgoe
> Father and Mother, and to his Wife adhere;
> And they shall be one Flesh, one Heart, one Soule.[22]

The dedication expressed here is so complete that it becomes a total identification; Adam and Eve are one, one flesh, one heart, one soul, in short, one person. Adam's dedication, then, is the result of sacrificing his reason or independent insight; he has no choice but to follow Eve. Such a sacrifice associates Adam with Milton, even though the objects of their dedication are strikingly different.

One can begin to see now why it is that when we come to the account of the Fall itself Adam's attachment to Eve serves to qualify, if not to undermine completely, the more general direction of the poem, "to justifie the wayes of God to men". Once Eve has succumbed to the wiles of the serpent what can Adam do except reaffirm that they are one?

> I feel
> The Link of Nature draw me: Flesh of Flesh,
> Bone of my Bone thou art, and from thy State
> Mine never shall be parted, bliss or woe . . .

and, some lines later,

> if Death
> Consort with thee, Death is to mee as Life;
> So forcible within my heart I feel
> The Bond of Nature draw me to my owne,

> My own in thee, for what thou art is mine;
> Our State cannot be severed, we are one,
> One Flesh; to loose thee were to loose my self.[23]

This is Adam, justifying his Fall and justifying it with all the assurance and majesty that Milton's verse can command. And here, it seems to me, Milton's sweeping confidence merges with that of Adam.

As one reads through Milton's account of the Fall in Book IX the pervading perplexities fail to resolve themselves into a recognition and convincing acceptance of human frailty; on the contrary, the trial of man which should have revealed the fatal weaknesses from which all our perplexities and doubts derive turns almost imperceptibly into a revelation of Adam's heroic integrity and courage. Indeed, what is put on trial, *is* that integrity, for he has to decide whether or not to reject Eve; Adam and Eve are "one Flesh, one Heart, one Soule" and, as Adam has already remarked to Eve, "to loose thee were to loose myself". Adam, then, in choosing not to lose Eve is choosing not to lose himself.

There is no doubt as to what the attitude towards the Fall ought to be. Adam has sinned and his sin is the consequence of his concupiscence; he has allowed the appeal of the flesh to over-ride his judgment. When Eve offers him the apple, we are told,

> he scrupl'd not to eat
> Against his better knowledge, not deceav'd,
> But fondly overcome with Female charm.[24]

It is from this more or less orthodox interpretation of the Fall of Man that Milton is able to extract such pleasant advice as,

> Thus it shall befall
> Him who to worth in Women overtrusting
> Lets her Will rule; restraint she will not brook,
> And left to her self, if evil thence ensue,
> Shee first his weak indulgence will accuse.[25]

It is in line with this interpretation that Adam explains his fall to the Son of God in Book X:

> This Woman whom Thou mad'st to be my help,
> And gav'st me as Thy perfet gift, so good,
> So fit, so acceptable, so Divine,
> That from her hand I could suspect no ill,
> And what she did, whatever in it self,

> Her doing seemed to justifie the deed;
> Shee gave me of the Tree, and I did eate.[26]

The Son of God accepts this account, which places the blame on God, but chides Adam for having allowed a woman to over-rule his better judgment.

This account of the Fall of Man is more impeccable theologically than the impression one receives of it as one reads through Books VIII and IX. The account itself, it will be noticed, is not entirely consistent. In Book IX (in the first passage quoted) we are told that Adam was "not deceav'd" and yet the excuse he offers to the Son of God is that he *was* deceived—"from her hand I could suspect no ill. Shee gave me of the Tree, and I did eate". This excuse is accepted in substance by the Son, who scolds Adam for allowing himself to be deceived not for lying. So much, it seems, for God's omniscience. However, the inconsistency which has the most profound effect upon the reader is that between the characterisation of Adam as he reaches his decision and the account we are given of this after the decision has been taken. We are told that Adam sins because he is "fondly overcome with Female charm". How true is this? Consider the lines in which Adam responds to Eve's suggestion that he should join with her in eating the apple:

> O fairest of Creation, last and best
> Of all Gods Works, Creature in whom excell'd
> Whatever can to sight or thought be formd,
> Holy, divine, good, amiable, or sweet!
> How art thou lost, how on a sudden lost,
> Defact't, deflour'd and now to Death devote?
> Rather how hast thou yeelded to transgress
> The strict forbiddance, how to violate
> The sacred Fruit forbidd'n! some cursed fraud
> of Enemie hath beguil'd thee, yet unknown,
> And mee with thee hath ruind, for with thee
> Certain my resolution is to Die;
> How can I live without thee, how forgoe
> Thy sweet Converse and Love so dearly joind,
> To live again in these wilde Woods forlorn?
> Should God create another Eve, and I
> Another Rib afford, yet loss of thee
> Would never from my heart; no, no, I feel
> The Link of Nature draw me: Flesh of Flesh,
> Bone of my Bone thou art, and from thy State
> Mine never shall be parted, bliss or woe.[27]

Then, having considered the possibility that God may not after all punish them as he had threatened, Adam concludes,

> However I with thee have fixt my lot,
> Certain to undergoe like doom; if Death
> Consort with thee, Death is to mee as Life;
> So forcible within my heart I feel
> The Bond of Nature draw me to my owne,
> My own in thee, for what thou art is mine;
> Our State cannot be served, we are one,
> One Flesh; to loose thee were to loose my self.[28]

This is surely the voice of a true, indeed an heroic love; it is hardly the voice of one "fondly overcome with Female charm". Eve is truer to the tone and attachment of Adam's lines when she replies, "O glorious trial of exceeding love".[29]

One can sum up the inconsistency in Milton's account by saying that what should have been a trial of Adam's love for God becomes a trial of his love for Eve and one from which Adam emerges victorious. The damage is irreparable and though the trial and the triumph is later represented as the defeat of a man "fondly overcome with Female charm" the judgment rings false. The same can be said of the attempt to transform the triumph into the triumph of lust. In other words, after the trial of Adam's love for Eve and Adam's victory, Milton attempts the impossible task of getting the account of the Fall back onto more or less orthodox rails, counterbalancing Adam's professed dedication to Eve with such lines as

> Nor onely Teares
> Raind at thir Eyes, but high Winds worse within
> Began to rise, high Passions, Anger, Hate,
> Mistrust, Suspicion, Discord, and shook sore
> Thir inward State of Mind, calme Region once
> And full of Peace, now tost and turbulent:
> For Understanding rul'd not, and the Will
> Heard not her lore, both in subjection now
> To sensual Appetite . . .[30]

The predicament remains: Adam could either turn from Eve, renouncing her and the bond that makes them one, in the interests of his own salvation, or he can heroically realise his love for her and in so doing transform his love into lust. The tragic predicament, then, is of a love that must either be betrayed or else be annihilated. Adam has little choice; since he and Eve are one he can no more reject her than he can himself. Furthermore, and much more to the point, in rejecting Eve Adam would have been rejecting his own humanity in favour of the pleasures of Eden and immortality. The whole conception (for which, of course, Milton was not responsible) and the whole execution (for which he was) of the trial of Adam is a chaos of conflicting attitudes and emotions from which Milton is unable to escape. There is the inexplicable degeneration of Adam's love into lust, the tragic paradox which confronts Adam at the moment of decision, and by a general implication there is the strong suggestion of a Deity ready to exact his pound of flesh, as though some all-powerful father was keeping close watch over his children, ready to pounce and put them to death for scrumping. Then there is the narrator, a kind of defence lawyer for the Deity, offering the bad character of the victims in excuse of his client's action.

It is not possible to turn from *Paradise Lost* without some considera-tion of the most controversial of Milton's characters, Satan. Yet it seems to me that Satan is of only peripheral interest in the action of the poem, the fall of Adam. In the action Satan is a device, a means of intruding into Eve's mind suggestions that are alien to her character, which (up to that point) is flawed only by a presumptuous indepen-dence. With spurious reasoning Satan leads Eve on to sin. Perhaps the most significant feature of this performance, however, is obscured by calling Satan's reasoning spurious; in itself it can hardly be faulted and Eve goes astray not because she accepts spurious reasoning as sound but because she allows reason to over-rule faith. She offends against the presumption of Milton's style, that a particular logic must surrender to a large assurance.

The characterisation of Satan is marked by the inconsistencies which stem from that surrender. He enters Eden and his eye is caught by the figure of his victim, Eve:

> Much he the Place admir'd, the Person more.
> As one who long in populous City pent,
> Where Houses thick and Sewers annoy the Aire,
> Forth issuing on a Summers Morn to breathe
> Among the pleasant Villages and Farmes
> Adjoind, from each thing met conceaves delight,
> The smell of Grain, or tedded Grass, or Kine,
> Or Dairie, each rural sight, each rural sound . . .[31]

There is a down-to-earth particularity and a fineness in these lines
(lines remembered perhaps in the opening of Wordworth's *Prelude*)
which associate Satan, appreciatively, with the natural and beneficently human activities of life. The passage continues, elaborating
upon Satan's appreciation of Eve:

> If chance with Nymphlike step fair Virgin pass,
> What pleasing seemd, for her now pleases more,
> Shee most, and in her look summs all Delight.
> Such Pleasure took the Serpent to behold
> This Flourie Plat, the sweet recess of Eve
> Thus earlie, thus alone; her Heav'nly forme
> Angelic, but more soft, and Feminine,
> Her graceful Innocence, her every Aire
> Of gesture or lest action overawd
> His Malice, and with rapin sweet bereav'd
> His fierceness of the fierce intent it brought:
> That space the Evil one abstracted stood
> From his own evil, and for the time remaind
> Stupidly good, of enmitie disarm'd,
> Of guile, of hate, of envie, of revenge . . .[32]

Evidently Satan is not entirely true to himself when he remarks, a few
lines later, that

> Save what is in destroying, other joy
> To mee is lost.[33]

This inconsistency, however, might be seen to have some point. If
the female charm of Eve can make Satan forget himself and stand
abstracted from his nature, how much more likely is she to have a
similarly devastating effect upon Adam. One can, then, look upon the
passage as a prolegomena to that in which Eve offers the apple to
Adam. It makes it more credible that Adam should be overcome by her
charms and so also makes more credible the excuse which Adam offers
to the Son of God.

There is a certain coherence in the passages I have been quoting: that
in which Adam confesses to Raphael the effect which Eve's appearance
has upon him and that in which Raphael warns him against this; that
in which Satan is abstracted from his evil at the sight of Eve; that
which explains Adam's fall in terms of his seduction by female charm;
and that in which Adam excuses himself to the Son of God by claim-
ing that he was taken in by Eve's appearance. These passages provide a

consistent account of the reasons for Adam's fall. But, intermixed with these, we have the passages of dedication in which Adam defines his relationship to Eve—"Bone of my Bone, Flesh of my Flesh, my Self". In these passages Eve's charms pass unrecognised and their relationship is established as something far more profound than one grounded in mere wiles and charms. It may be that the answer to Raphael's question to Adam.

> For what admir'st thou, what transports thee so,
> An outside?

is yes. That may well be what Adam admires. But when it comes to the test it is not in terms of admiration that Adam's decision is made. It is a decision based upon a more profound recognition of their common nature, their common humanity.

> I feel
> The Link of Nature draw me,

Adam observes, and a little later,

> I feel
> The Bond of Nature draw me to my owne.

Milton, then, is providing two inconsistent accounts of the Fall of Man; the one affirming Adam's uxoriousness and the other his common humanity. The perplexity remains, that pervasive perplexity which is realised at large in Milton's style and springs from a corresponding state of mind and feeling. Instead of resolving this, Milton's account of the Fall of Man allegorises a sense of sin at loggerheads with a sense of common humanity. In this *Paradise Lost* yet again expresses the perplexities besetting the Puritan consciousness of the time. The first great democratic experiment had failed. Why had it? Surely because God had deserted us for our sins. But how had we sinned in asserting common humanity? The question is unanswerable and could only have puzzled people who thought, as did the vast majority of Milton's contemporaries, of society as a Christian community and of the democratic revolution as a Puritan Reformation. The democratic revolution was concerned with humanity; the Puritan Reformation with sin and salvation.

What one can perceive in Milton's account of the Fall of Man is something of the conflict between two views of the nature of man, a conflict between man as essentially noble, heroic and courageous and man as essentially weak and sinful, between confidence in man and lack of confidence in him. And looking back upon the Revolution one can detect the roots of its failure in the growth of the latter, in a growing suspicion of the mass of ordinary people, of the rank of file of the Army in particular, by the leadership. The revolutionary ebullience of the common people was checked and castigated as sinful, their morale undermined and infiltrated by a sense of guilt, or rather of sin. It is not by accident that the passage which describes Satan's first view of Eve associates him appreciatively with the natural, spontaneous and beneficently human responses to fresh life: it marks the growing distrust of the increased freedom and buoyancy of common life. Is it any wonder, then, that Satan should have been felt by so many readers of *Paradise Lost* to be not simply heroically evil but also heroically human?

2. THE POPULARITY OF 'THE PILGRIM'S PROGRESS'

John Bunyan and John Milton were both Nonconformists but Nonconformists of entirely different temper and talent, a fact which assumes considerable significance in their major works. The relationship between *Paradise Lost* and *The Pilgrim's Progress* is nicely indicated in their titles, in Milton's sense of loss and Bunyan's awareness of something still to be achieved. As expressions of seventeenth-century nonconformity they are in many respects complementary opposites: Milton's epic reflects the quietism which permeated many of the nonconformist sects after the defeat of the Revolution, whilst Bunyan's prose odyssey expresses the continuing resolution of others to confront and do battle with the evils of this world. Milton chronicles the fall of man; Bunyan the spiritual calibre and progress of the resolute soul in a fallen world. If Milton's great poem is inspired by the failure to build Jerusalem in England's green and pleasant land and by the perplexities to which this failure gave rise in the Puritan mind, Bunyan's powerful parable is intent upon charting a path through the ruins and banishing all perplexities with a confident reaffirmation of militant dissent.

Something of Bunyan's character is gathered when, as Offor remarked,

> It is recollected that Bunyan received the most imperfect rudiments of education in a charity school when very young, which were "almost entirely" obliterated by bad habits—that he was a hardworking man through life, maintaining himself, a wife, and four children, by his severe labour as a brazier—and yet, by personal

efforts, he educated himself and wrote sixty-two valuable religious treatises, numbering among them his inimitable allegories, *The Pilgrim's Progress*, and *Holy War*, made a Concordance to the Bible, and conducted important controversies. Preaching, while at liberty, almost innumerable sermons on the Lord's-days and week-days, early in the morning and late at night. Visiting his flock with pastoral care—founding churches in the villages, and even in towns and cities far distant from his dwelling—constantly giving advice to promote peace and good will, and rendering benevolent aid by long journeys! His whole life presents to us a picture of most astonishing, energetic perseverance.[1]

It is such an energetic perseverance that is epitomised in the hero of *Pilgrim's Progress*.

Werner Pelz once gave a talk on the B.B.C. Third Programme entitled *On Being a Parable* (20 August 1963) in which he pointed out that "Traditionally a parable has been held to be 'an earthly story with a heavenly meaning'". In this sense we may be inclined to think of John Bunyan's *The Pilgrim's Progress* as a parable. In a dream Bunyan's narrator sees Christian, on the advice of Evangelist, flee from the City of Destruction, and follows him upon his journey through the Slough of Despond, the Valley of Humiliation, the Valley of the Shadow of Death, the Delectable Mountains, the country of Beulah, and finally, after many trials and vicissitudes, across the River of Death to the Celestial City. The second part, with which I am not concerned, relates how Christian's wife, Christiana, moved by a vision, sets out with her children and her good neighbour Mercy upon the same journey.

As befits an English parable, the topography of *The Pilgrim's Progress* is plainly English. Christian's journey along the straight and narrow path lies through the English countryside of the seventeenth century, with its bogs, meadows, orchards, vineyards (common in southern England then), its crooked lanes, castles, occasional cliffs, hostelries, gates and stiles, rivers and streams. But the allegorical nature of Bunyan's countryside, obvious enough in the place names, is more complex than we would suppose were we simply to pursue its heavenly meaning. It is a countryside steeped not only in Christian belief but also in the fears, both real and imaginary, of any poor traveller of the time—fears of thieves, goblins, dragons, giants. The journey upon which Christian sets out, therefore, is one through the English country-side as this has been invested by the popular imagination with real dangers and old superstitions partially translated into figures of Christian belief. It is this characteristic of the work which enables us to make an initial distinction between Christian's belief, with its roots in folk lore, and Christian belief; it is the distinction between earthly story and heavenly meaning. And it is, I think, to the ambivalence of the popular and biblical that we must turn in order to understand the great popularity which *The Pilgrim's Progress* enjoyed until the end of the last century.

Until late in the nineteenth century two books underlay the popular culture of England; one was the Authorised Version of the Bible and the other was Bunyan's *The Pilgrim's Progress*. I mean 'underlay' quite particularly: before the coming of universal education, working-class people in England commonly learned to read from one or the other of these books and often from both. They became the two great idiomatic works of popular English; they coloured popular speech with biblical and Bunyanesque turns of phrase, and behind the habits of speech which they instilled lay habits of thought and attitude. The poor in particular were disposed by Bunyan to look upon life as a struggle in which, ultimately, they could prevail, as those of wealth and privilege were likely to be lost eternally amidst the things of this world.

This sounds quietistic; one recalls that Bunyan was a Baptist and that the Baptists are often said to have become quietistic after the Restoration. And indeed the immediate lesson which Bunyan's parable appears to set before us is that of the value of patience and fortitude in the face of the temptations and ill-usage of the world. To the poor, therefore, it would seem to preach, "Bear thy lot in patience and think on the world to come." This is the lesson unfolded before Christian in the House of the Interpreter. When the Interpreter shows Christian two little children seated on chairs, one discontented and the other quiet and calm, he explains to Christian that

> These two lads are figures: Passion, of the men of this world; and Patience, of the men of that which is to come; for, as here thou seest, Passion will have all now this year, that is to say, in this world; so are the men of this world: they must have all their good things now, they cannot stay till next year, that is, until the next world, for their portion of good. That proverb, "A bird in the hand is worth two in the bush", is of more authority with them than are all the Divine testimonies of the good of the world to come. But as thou sawest that he had quickly lavished all away, and had presently

left him nothing but rags; so it will be with all such men at the end of this world.

Then said Christian, Now I see that Patience has the best wisdom, and that upon many accounts. First, Because he stays for the best things. Second, And also because he will have the glory of his, when the other has nothing but rags.

Upon which the Interpreter remarks,

Nay, you may add another, to wit, the glory of the next world will never wear out; but these are suddenly gone. Therefore Passion had not so much reason to laugh at Patience, because he had his good things first, as Patience will have to laugh at Passion, because he had his best things last.

And Christian concludes,

Then I perceive it is not best to covet things that are now, but to wait for things to come.[2]

The overall effect of *The Pilgrim's Progress*, however, is closer to the spirit of Bunyan himself, the tinsmith who served in the ranks of the Commonwealth army, as he lay in Bedford prison after the Restoration. It is of a piece with the man who, at his trial, when Justice Keeling informed him that unless he gave over preaching he would be banished and upon his return be hung by the neck, replied, "If I was out of prison to-day I would preach the gospel again tomorrow, by the help of God."[3] The general impression created by *The Pilgrim's Progress*, that is to say, is not one of quietism and defeat but of stubborn and unflinching courage: truly one should be prepared to suffer, for this was the lot of those who chose the straight and narrow path, and no one who had chosen that path ought to allow himself to be deflected by suffering and poverty, on the one hand, or by the promise of the things of this world, on the other.

This world, the world of Restoration England, is set before us microcosmically in the well-to-do market town of Vanity Fair. Passing through the town, Christian and his companion Faithful are arrested for disturbing the peace and are eventually brought to trial. The charge against them is in essence that brought against so many dissenting 'mechanic preachers' in the courts of Restoration England and one which places the shop stewards of our own day in a tradition stretching back through the Tolpuddle Martyrs to Bunyan and his comrades. It is

That they were enemies to, and disturbers of their trade; that they made commotions and divisions in the town, and had won a party to their own dangerous opinions, in contempt of the law of their prince.[4]

In the course of the trial we learn from the witness Pickthank that Faithful

hath railed on our noble prince Beelzebub, and hath spoken contemptibly of his honourable friends, whose names are the Lord Old Man, the Lord Carnal Delight, the Lord Luxurious, the Lord Desire of Vain Glory, my old Lord Lechery, Sir Having Greedy, with all the rest of our nobility. . . . Besides, he hath not been afraid to rail on you, my Lord, who are now appointed to be his judge, calling you an ungodly villain, with many other such like vilifying terms, with which he hath bespattered most of the gentry of our town.[5]

In reply to which charge Faithful admits quite readily that he had indeed maintained

That the prince of this town, with all the rabblement, his attendants, by this gentleman named, are more fit for a being in hell, than in this town and country.[6]

The revolutionary character of this attack upon the aristocracy and gentry of Restoration England, and the 'justice' administered by them, is sustained throughout Bunyan's magnificent description of the trial: this represents royalist England as seen by a revolutionary Puritan.* It is little wonder that, professing such opinions, the Bedford preacher was thrown into prison. It should be remarked, however, that the trial and incarceration of Christian does not draw specifically upon the experience of Bunyan but rather on the common experience of English dissenters following the Restoration, many tens of thousands of whom were imprisoned for their beliefs; and though none were burned, as was Faithful, yet many were hung, as was John James, pastor of the Baptist church in Whitechapel, and many thousand others, men women and children, died or were brutally tortured and done to death in prison. Picart's *Religious Ceremonies* computed the number of dissenters who died in prison during the reign of Charles II as 8,000, most of whom seem to have been murdered by their captors.[7]

* Macaulay makes the same point in reviewing Southey's edition of *The Pilgrim's Progress* (Macaulay, I, 285–6)

We may be tempted to describe such passages as those which deal with the trial as satiric. Unlike Pope, however, whose satire proceeds from the ideal of a purified aristocracy, and Swift, who is a cynic, Bunyan's criticism of the contemporary scene springs directly from his championship of the righteous poor. Unlike the satirist, Bunyan is not limited to a doctrine of reform. His championship is quite explicit: Christ, we are informed at one point,

> is such a lover of poor pilgrims, that the like is not to be found from the east to the west . . . he had stripped himself of his glory, that he might do this for the poor; and they had heard him say and affirm 'that he would not dwell in the mountain of Zion alone.'*[8]

At another point, Christian prepares to do battle with the dragon Apollyon, because, as he remarks, "your service was hard, and your wages such as man could not live on".[9] We hear of Shame's objections to Faithful; one of the most important of these, Faithful informs us, is

> that but few of the mighty, rich or wise, were ever of my opinion. . . . He, moreover, objected the base and low estate and condition of those that were chiefly the pilgrims of the times in which they lived; also their ignorance, and want of understanding in all natural science.[10]

None of which is ever denied. It is an objection which reminds us not only of the ignorance of the sectarians but of the fact that, "by substituting the written word of the Scriptures for the hierarchy as the final authority in religious life, Puritanism took the effective direction of religious affairs from the hands of the prelates only to make it the monopoly of a literate, educated class. The reply of the poor—and hence, the illiterate and uneducated—was that not formal learning but an inner spiritual experience and inspiration were the true source of religious knowledge."[11] Bunyan, indeed, places a particular emphasis upon the ignorance of his pilgrims. When Christian and Hopeful, Christian's companion in the latter half of his journey after the execu-

---

* In *A Few Sighs from Hell* this same championship of the poor leads Bunyan to reject the Puritan doctrine of the calling.

Do but ask a poor, carnal, covetous wretch, how we should know a man to be in a happy state, and he will answer, those that God blesseth, and giveth abundance of this world unto; when, for the most part, they are they that are the cursed men. Alas! poor men, they are so ignorant as to think that because a man is increased in outward things, and that by a small stock, therefore God doth love that man with a special love, or else he would never do so much for him, never bless him so, and prosper the work of his hands. Ah! poor soul, it is the rich man that goes to hell. (Offor, III, 675.)

tion of Faithful, arrive at the pillar into which Lot's wife had been transformed they wonder what it is.

At last Hopeful espied written above the head thereof, a writing in an unusual hand; but he being no scholar, called to Christian (for he was learned) to see if he could pick out the meaning; so he came, and after a little laying of letters together, he found the same to be this, "Remember Lot's wife". So he read it to his fellow.[12]

Such difficulties in reading a public inscription, intended as a guide to poor pilgrims, admits to the ignorance charged against them by Shame; it is the ignorance of the unlettered poor. And what Shame finally deplores is that religion makes the religious man "own and respect the base". To which Faithful retorts "that the poor man that loveth Christ is richer than the greatest man in the world that hates him".*[13]

I have quoted fairly extensively in order to make the point that no amount of jibing at Marxist criticism, such as Dr. Leavis once indulged himself in when reviewing Jack Lindsay's book on Bunyan, can eradicate from *The Pilgrim's Progress* passages so evidently there, expressing Bunyan's realisation of the opposition between the poor, "that were chiefly the pilgrims of the times in which they lived", and the 'rabblement' of the gentry and the aristocracy. Whilst impertinent criticism distracts the attention, it cannot erase from *The Pilgrim's Progress* its justification of the righteous poor as an elect and its lesson of courage in the face of the powers-that-be. In significant contrast to the epic of Milton, with its intention "to justifie the wayes of God to men", Bunyan gives a powerful and compelling form to the conviction that the poor shall inherit the earth.

Unless we appreciate the revolutionary spirit of *The Pilgrim's Progress* the greatness of the work will elude us. Milton's greatness is apparent: he helped to fashion the consciousness and sensibility of polite society

---

* Bunyan himself was what Eliot calls "one of the low". In *Grace Abounding* he informs us that "My descent . . . was, as is well known by many, of a low and inconsiderable generation, my father's house being of that rank that is meanest and most despised of all the families in the land" (Offor, I, 6). In controversy he rounds upon the Strict Baptists since, as he charges them, "you closely disdain my person because of my low descent among men, stigmatizing me as a person of THAT rank that need not be heeded or attended unto" (Offor, II, 617). To all such he gives his reply in *The Fear of God*: 'The Poor Christian hath something to answer them that reproach him for his ignoble pedigree, and shortness of the glory of the wisdom of this world. True, may that man say, I am taken out of the dunghill, I was born in a base and low estate, but I fear God. This is the highest and most noble; he hath the honour, the life, and glory that is lasting" (Offor, I, 490).

throughout the eighteenth and nineteenth centuries. His greatness has been perpetuated not in the "simple annals of the poor" but in the calf-bound volumes of the rich. Bunyan, on the other hand, fashioned the consciousness and sensibilities of those whose labour and poverty supported the dubious civilisation of the *beau monde*. As George Offor observed in his edition of Bunyan,

> the works of Bunyan, which have been the most popular of all books . . . were for many years so exclusively patronized by the poor, as to have been most humbly and imperfectly published.
>
> Even that singularly popular book, *The Pilgrim's Progress*, was meanly printed in separate parts for half a century, on paper of the worst quality—in the cheapest form—with the rudest cuts. Innumerable copies of these were sold to the poor, and have been so devoured and worn out, as to have become rare in proportion to their age. . . . His other treatises were most numerously but inelegantly published for the use of the poor; and the early editions, like those of *The Pilgrim's Progress*, have been so worn out with fair but hard use, as to have become exceedingly scarce and difficult of access. Their contents were devoured by anxious readers, far more desirous to store up in their minds the sacred truths they contained, then to preserve the little books which were so blessed to them.[14]

Both Milton and Bunyan were men of the Revolution, of course, but the rebellion in *Paradise Lost* is an abstract affair, universal perhaps (although *Pilgrim's Progress* has been translated into most languages and *Paradise Lost* into few) but set in a distant past, at the very beginning of time, and in a country far removed from England. The rebelliousness of *The Pilgrim's Progress*, for its part, is specifically English, set in seventeenth-century England, amidst its society of lords, gentry, merchants, and poor. Bunyan's work celebrates the Revolution with a justification of the struggles of the rank and file. Milton translates the struggles of the time into abstract disputes, making the spirit of the revolt 'safe'. Some intimation of the difference in spirit, as I have already mentioned, can be gathered from the *Lost* of Milton's title and the *Progress* of Bunyan's.

But Bunyan's work would not have been capable of sustaining and giving form and substance to the lives and aspirations of the poor did it not itself possess qualities of greatness commensurable with such a rôle. It is, after all, not doctrine alone that can explain its power to educate and make literate and articulate generation after generation of the common people, and it was certainly not the doctrine of *The*

Pilgrim's Progress which led Dr. Johnson to praise it so highly.[15] In our own time Bunyan's work has been said to have a certain child-like quality. And although Miss Bennett, who made this observation in her book on the metaphysical poets when comparing Bunyan and Herbert,[16] does not go on to amplify it, it is plain enough what she had in mind. As I have already suggested, although the countryside of *The Pilgrim's Progress* is English, it is viewed through the popular imagination of the time as a place beset for the traveller with a variety of dangers, such as giants, dragons, devils, witches, goblins and the like. It is, in brief, the England out of which the ballads and folk stories grew. Consider, for instance, the description of the monster Apollyon:

> Now the monster was hideous to behold; he was clothed with scales, like a fish (and they are his pride), he had wings like a dragon, feet like a bear, and out of his belly came fire and smoke, and his mouth was as the mouth of a lion.[17]

There is here, in the actual writing, more than a little of that open-mouthed awe which must have been felt by generations of children as they sat around the fireside and listened to the adventures of Christian. We are not surprised to learn from Macaulay that "in every nursery, the Pilgrim's Progress is a greater favourite than Jack the Giant-Killer".[18] But child-like awe is not the sum-total of our response to *The Pilgrim's Progress*, as it might be to a fairy tale. It serves to invest the figure of Christian with the aura of popular imagination, making the pilgrim into something of a folk hero, a figure capable of evoking and associating with those popular feelings that clothe themselves in folk lore. This touches the roots of the book's popular appeal; it is an appeal to the past as it lives in the imaginations of the people and which gives to that other and more specific past, the past of the Revolution, a strong link with the folk-lore world of popular culture.

This is not, of course, to deny the important influence of the Bible upon the writing of Bunyan. Apollyon, for instance, is the fallen angel mentioned in Revelation ix:11 and Bunyan's description of his monster echoes that of the seven-headed beast of Revelation (xiii:2):

> And the beast which I saw was like unto a leopard, and his feet were as the feet of a bear, and his mouth as the mouth of a lion; and the dragon gave him his power. . . .

Nevertheless the formative vision of *The Pilgrim's Progress* is that of popular culture. The Bible itself grew out of that culture and the beast of Revelation is present in *The Pilgrim's Progress* because it belongs to the marvellous world of folk lore. At the time, no doubt, the Biblical allusions would have produced a more complex response than this suggests. In Puritan mythology, for instance, the seven-headed beast of Revelation had long represented that monster of prelacy and social reaction which enslaved Europe from its den in the city of the seven hills, Rome. So that the beast of folk-lore takes upon itself a more particular and historical significance which again links the world of folk lore with that of popular struggle.

In Bunyan the popular vision, which gives a childlike (but not a childish) quality to the prose, is a continuous strength. It is most evident in the manner in which the fantastic is seen in terms of everyday routine; in, for instance, the domesticity with which Giant Despair is presented reviewing the day's problems with his wife as they lie in bed at Doubting Castle—

> Now, when night was come, and when Mrs. Diffidence and her husband, the Giant, were got to bed . . .[19]

The same domesticity is there in the Giant's obedience to his wife. His wife said he must search the pilgrims,

> And sayest thou so, my dear? said the Giant; I will, therefore, search them in the morning,[20]

and he shows the pilgrims the bones stacked in the back-yard "as his wife has bidden him". What gives the parable of Despair its peculiar air of familiarity is its homely vision of the ogre as a hen-pecked husband and the consummate ease with which Bunyan maintains the tone of the popular raconteur or gossip, "Well, on Saturday, about midnight . . ."

The best description of Bunyan's prose is that provided by Macaulay.

> The style of Bunyan is delightful to every reader, and invaluable as a study to every person who wishes to obtain a wide command over the English language. The vocabulary is the vocabulary of the common people. There is not an expression, if we except a few technical terms of theology, which would puzzle the rudest peasant. We have observed several pages which do not contain a single word of more than two syllables. Yet no writer has said more exactly what he meant to say. For magnificence, for pathos, for vehement exhortation, for subtle disquisition, for every purpose of the poet, the orator, and the divine, this homely dialect, the dialect of plain working men,—was perfectly sufficient. There is no book in our

literature on which we would so readily stake the fame of the old unpolluted English language,—no book which shows so well how rich that language is in its own proper wealth, and how little it has been improved by all that is has borrowed.[21]

Compare the style of Bunyan, as Macaulay has so well described it, with the pomp and circumstance of Milton's style, so abstract, so remote, grandiloquent and learnedly abstruse; nothing could be farther removed from Bunyan's English. One is never led to wonder at the character of Bunyan's prose, although frequently led to wonder by it; one is never tempted to question the familiarity with which it invests the fantastic. This is partly because the fantastic has in itself the familiarity of folk lore, a familiarity upon which Bunyan's style is based. But also, and connected with this, because his prose is grounded in the familiarity of spoken English: "Bunyan", Macaulay remarked, "is almost the only writer that ever gave to the abstract the interest of the concrete."[22]

One of Molière's characters expresses great surprise when informed that he speaks in prose, having been under the impression that prose was written not spoken. No one reading Bunyan would be surprised on being told this; his "dialect of plain working men", for all its apparent simplicity and artlessness, involves and gains its strength from ranges of English life that are inimical to the 'refinement' (with all the social implications that word has) that expresses itself in the careful cultivation of a prose style. It is the vehicle of a specifically English popular culture, a culture to which we must look in trying to account for the courage, the commitments and the greatness of *The Pilgrim's Progress*.

5

Johnson: Shakespeare and the Prince of Abyssinia

I. JOHNSON ON SHAKESPEARE

It is necessary but not sufficient for criticism to place past literature in the past, recognising the limitations of consciousness described by the beliefs and modes of thinking of a bygone age. Criticism implies self-criticism and the recognition that we ourselves are often in the control of opinions which derive from large historical presumptions. It may be objected that this line of thinking leads eventually to critical relativism and a final refusal to judge. But in a sense all criticism is relative in that it is related to specific conditions of life which do in fact change. If criticism is not relativistic in an agnostic sense it is because the conditions of life and the standards of criticism are not accidental; change is real but it is not fortuitous. This sounds perilously close to an historical abstraction, but Johnson's *Preface to Shakespeare* provides an opportunity to render the generalisation as a specific observation.

Johnson's *Preface to Shakespeare* is an essay particularly well-suited to illustrating what Karl Jaspers has called the "inescapable attachment of oneself to one's age at a particular place".[1] Macaulay, a great but commonly underestimated critic of Johnson, remarked of Johnson that "he judged of all works of the imagination by the standards established among his contemporaries" and so "preferred Pope's Iliad to Homer's". "It is remarkable," he added, "that to the last he entertained a fixed contempt for all those modes of life and those studies which tend to emancipate the mind from the prejudices of a particular age or a particular nation."[2]

Macaulay quite plainly and rightly believes that the writer is not necessarily in servitude to his age; Johnson, on the other hand, believes that "it is seldom that authors, though more studious of fame than Shakespeare, rise much above the standard of their own age"[3] and frequently excuses Shakespeare's faults by reference to the age in which he lived. Johnson is, of course, and characteristically, over-simplifying matters in favouring such a relativistic view, for men, whether studious of fame or not, display a large variety of attitudes towards the standards and opinions peculiar to their age, ranging as they do from absolute acceptance to total rejection. Johnson himself professes to be ignorant of prevailing opinion at one point—

> To the end of most plays, I have added short strictures, containing a general censure of faults, or praise of excellence; in which I know not how much I have concurred with the current opinion[4]

—but his attitude towards it as he hurries to disclaim, "but I have not, by an affectation of singularity, deviated from it", is far removed from that of Swift. It is the deference revealed in such a disclaimer that largely controls Johnson's style. Consider, as an illustration of this, the opening paragraph of the *Preface*, the one which, as we read it, sets the tone and disposes the reader towards what is to follow:

> That praises are without reason lavished on the dead, and that the honours due only to excellence are paid to antiquity, is a complaint likely to be always continued by those, who, being able to add nothing to truth, hope for eminence from the heresies of paradox; or those, who, being forced by disappointment upon consolatory expedients, are willing to hope from posterity what the present age refuses, and flatter themselves that the regard which is yet denied by envy, will be at last bestowed by time.[5]

Johnson here, in dismissing a complaint and a presumption that have often been justified, comes forward as a champion of the standards of his age; one might represent the general appeal quite minutely by drawing attention to the phrase "the heresies of paradox" and by asking why the complaint is considered paradoxical and, more to the point, by reflecting that in describing paradox as heretical Johnson uncompromisingly aligns himself with orthodox or received opinion.

If Johnson's style is weighty, then, it is so in the sense that it has behind it the weight of common or received opinion. The presumption of such support is what gives to his prose its air of unruffled certainty, lending to his considerations the invariable force of public proclamation. But having said this it needs to be added that common opinion is necessarily a period piece and one which defines an age much more precisely than do many of its intellectual achievements. In saying that Johnson's commonsense is a period piece what I have in mind are those many pronouncements throughout the *Preface* which, for all their self-assurance, strike us as being either wrong or else beside

K

the point. The reason for dismissing them as wrong are almost as various as the pronouncements themselves. When, for instance, he remarks of Shakespeare that

> He sacrifices virtue to convenience, and is so much more careful to please than to instruct, that he seems to write without any moral purpose

and goes on to conclude,

> This fault the barbarity of his age cannot extenuate; for it is always a writer's duty to make the world better, and justice is a virtue independent on time or place . . . ,[6]

we are enmeshed in a tangled web of presumption which Johnson himself never appears to be conscious of at all. The character of the writing is, of course, such as to exclude reflection, but once reflection is brought to bear upon it the result is not an inner-assurance reinforcing the writing under review but a bewilderment that beats against it in vain. How is it possible for anyone who has read the conclusion of *King Lear*, and has read it as carefully as Johnson did, to charge Shakespeare with being "more careful to please than to instruct"? To whatever convenience Cordelia is sacrificed it is surely not that of pleasure. Similarly, to feel pleased at the death of Ophelia, Desdemona and Lady Macduff, and at the plight of Richard, Falstaff and Malvolio, one must possess a most peculiar capacity for pleasure. There is, one cannot escape feeling, something wrong here with Johnson's sensibilities, a fault informing the quality of the prose and giving to it a certain callousness. Similar observations can be made about his remark that Shakespeare "seems to write without any moral purpose". *Macbeth* may be, as Professor L. C. Knights has claimed,[7] a statement of evil, but if so it is a highly ambiguous one since it also affirms the ineluctable triumph of good. Surely in reading *Macbeth* one is aware above all of the moral struggle, the conflict of good and evil, expressing itself most completely in those passages most commonly remembered. It is of no critical consequence whether this was or was not Shakespeare's "moral purpose" since it is so plainly the play's effect.

That Johnson should appear so impervious to the moral purport of Shakespeare casts a light upon Johnson. I think, however, that it is an oblique light; that we can safely assume Johnson to have been fully aware of the moral effect of *Macbeth* but to have been dissatisfied with it. His criticism of Shakespeare, that he writes without any moral purpose, stems, I feel from his own belief that an adequate moral purpose is necessarily explicit, that it addresses itself directly to the reader's approbation in the manner of Coleridge towards the end of the Ancient Mariner.*

Now this Shakespeare seldom does; the moral appraisals created by Shakespeare are complex and inhere in particular dramatic situations. When, as on some notable occasions, we are loaded with precepts, as we are by Ulysses and Polonius, these have a hollow ring; they are too glib, too lacking in subtlety and finesse to apply to the situations which Shakespeare has created in *Troilus and Cressida* and *Hamlet*. Johnson, then, is not satisfied with the intrinsically moral cast of Shakespeare's work and feels a need for simpler and more explicit statements of the moral position.

The conclusion to be drawn from this is that Johnson is impervious to the nuances of judgment that make the problems of practical morality so infinitely complex.† Why cannot Macbeth be condemned outright as evil? Surely because an essential precept of an adequate morality is that of understanding and limited sympathy, of being able to call into consideration that "there, but for the Grace of God, go I". This consideration complicates the moral situation, the situation in which one has to judge of good and evil, enormously.

In this instance one can see something of the price that Johnson has to pay for his assurance. It is the price of over-simplifying, of taking life, and the situations with which life confronts us, too crudely. And reading through the *Preface* one can remark how often the assurance is allied to this crudity. It is there, for example, when Johnson writes that

> Those whom my arguments cannot persuade to give their approbation to the judgment of Shakespeare, will easily, if they consider the condition of his life, make some allowance for his ignorance.[8]

For his ignorance of what? His ignorance of the variety and complexity of life or of the relative simplicities of eighteenth century opinion as these are reflected in Johnson?

We may begin, then, by an observation of certain points of style,

* He prayeth best, who loveth best
  All things both great and small;
  For the dear God who loveth us,
  He made and loveth all.

† But see Macaulay (I, 389): "If he had been content to write as he talked, he might have left books on the practical art of living superior to the Directions to Servants."

indicative of a certain disposition or cast of mind and, hence, of values
deeply entrenched within the quality of Johnson's prose; but we must
continually turn to a point of time and a set of complacently held
assumptions:* life was essentially a simple business, to be regulated by
explicit rules. It is a life which can achieve expression in the platitudes
encountered in *Rasselas*. And, recognising this, recognising it in the
weighty crudities of Johnson's style, we come to see in his prose a kind
of life which is in many ways inadequate. Indeed, Johnson, in writing
of Shakespeare, deliberately exposes the life which he himself represents so well—its arrogance, complacency, limited commonsense and
crude desire for platitudinous rules of conduct—to a comparison with
the kind of life which informs Shakespeare.

Johnson deliberately provokes such a comparison (not, he believes,
to the detriment of his own age) in many of the quotations already
given; the challenge may be crystallised by yet another one:

> The English nation, in the time of Shakespeare was yet struggling
> to emerge from barbarity.[9]

It will be agreed, I think, that all Johnson's characteristic assurance is
there in that pronouncement, all his sense of unquestionable superiority if not to Shakespeare then to the "barbarity of his age". And we
hardly need to be reminded how obtuse such a statement is whether
considered as a description or as a judgment of the civilisation which
produced Shakespeare, Jonson, Donne. But the gauntlet is down and
one cannot finally place Johnson's *Preface* without measuring the civilisation instanced in the qualities of Johnson's prose alongside that to
which Shakespeare's poetry bears witness. It is well to remember also
that the charge of barbarism is not one which Johnson reserves for the
age of Shakespeare. Macaulay deplores the narrowness of outlook
revealed in Johnson's imputations of barbarity:

> "The Athenians of the age of Demosthenes," Johnson said to Mrs.
> Thrale, "were a people of brutes, a barbarous people." In conversa-
> tion with Sir Adam Ferguson he used similar language. "The boasted
> Athenians," he said, "were barbarians. The mass of every people
> must be barbarous where there is no printing." The fact was this: he
> saw that a Londoner who could not read was a very stupid and brutal
> fellow: he saw that great refinement of taste and activity of intellect

---

* "His whole code of criticism rested on pure assumption, for which he sometimes
quoted a precedent or an authority but rarely troubled himself to give a reason drawn
from the nature of things" (Macaulay, I, 387).

were rarely found in a Londoner who had not read much; and, because it was by means of books that people acquired almost all their knowledge in the society with which he was acquainted, he concluded, in defiance of the strongest and clearest evidence, that the human mind can be cultivated by means of books alone.[10]

Whilst enthralled to a particular time and place, Johnson's is a mind that shies away from the concrete and the particular and finds its aptest expression in generalisation and abstraction; this is a characteristic of eighteenth-century common sense, or rather of eighteenth-century rationalism, which pervades the judgments we meet with in the *Preface*. If Shakespeare is lasting it is not, in Johnson's estimation, as a representative of a particular kind of civilisation but because his work embodies abstract virtues:

As his personages act upon principles arising from genuine passion, very little modified by particular forms, their pleasures and vexations are communicable to all times and to all places; they are natural, and therefore durable; the adventitious peculiarities of personal habits are only superficial dies, bright and pleasing for a little while, yet soon fading to a dim tinct, without any remains of former lustre: but the discriminations of true passion are the colours of nature; they pervade the whole mass, and can only perish with the body that exhibits them.[11]

It ought by now to be a commonplace that Shakespeare's 'passions', as Johnson calls them, are quite particular, they are particularised by the context of the play of which they form a part, by our response to the complex whole; we err in abstracting the passions from their forms and occasions, in failing to realise that Shakespeare's particulars are vitally relevant. But I would also draw attention to that phrase, of the passions, "they are natural and therefore durable". Just as for Plato the real world is the world of Ideas, so for Johnson the natural world is the world of durable abstractions. But the natural world, as we understand it, is far from durable; even human nature is subject to the processes of change however ossified may be the terms to which we resort in order to discuss it.

This, then, is something essential to be grasped in reading Johnson: the pervasive belief that what is abstract is natural and what is natural is durable, whereas what is concrete is subject to decay and is, in some consequent sense, unnatural. It is essential to grasp this because it bears directly upon what has been observed of Johnson's style, its tendency towards generalisation, to over-simplify and, hence to crudify life and the problems of living in a world that is, for most of us, enormously complex, as it is in Shakespeare.* Now we can see the philosophic under-pinning of this style. And so, just as earlier we were called upon to compare the qualities of life represented by Johnson and Shakespeare, eighteenth-century and Elizabethan England, so now we are called upon to judge in matters of philosophy.

There is no need to go into the arguments for and against philo-sophic idealism; it is sufficient to observe that is an essential element in that rationalism already noted as instinct in Johnson's prose. As to the problems of judgment in this matter, it is only necessary to observe that this particular piece of philosophic idealism is itself an expression of those Johnsonian disabilities already remarked, an expression of that attenuation of life which becomes apparent when we consider the qualities of Johnson's prose and the civilisation it represents so strik-ingly (the limitations of which emerge most sharply when we com-pare it with that of Shakespeare).

It is this Johnsonian tendency to deal with the world, in this instance the world of Shakespeare, in terms of ideas, of abstractions—albeit moral abstractions—which accounts in some degree for that distortion of sensibility most clearly apparent when he is discussing such things as the distinction between tragedy and comedy in Shakespeare. "In tragedy," Johnson comments, Shakespeare

> often writes with great appearance of toil and study, what is written at last with little felicity; but in his comick scenes, he seems to produce without labour, what no labour can improve. In tragedy he is always struggling after some occasion to be comick, but in comedy he seems to repose, or to luxuriate, as in a mode of thinking congenial to his nature. In his tragick scenes there is always something wanting, but his comedy often surpasses expectations or desire. His comedy pleases by the thoughts and the language, and his tragedy for the greater part by incident and action. His tragedy seems to be skill, his comedy to be instinct.[12]

* Not every one would agree. For some there is a distinction to be made between the coarseness of response evoked by actual life and the delicacy of art. "We shall gain nothing," according to Wilson Knight, "by applying to the delicate symbols of the poet's imagination the rough machinery of an ethical philosophy created to control the turbulence of actual life" (G. Wilson Knight, *The Wheel of Fire*, London, 1949, p. 11). A rough ethical machinery, however, is no more adequate to "the turbulence of actual life" than it is to "the delicate symbols of the poet's imagination". To think otherwise is to have less respect and regard for your treatment of others than for your treatment of a book or a painting and that is to treat art as a fetish.

The passage is a fine illustration of what Macaulay called Johnson's "antithetical forms of expression".[13] Furthermore, and this is the point of the quotation, the distinction which is being made in the passage seems primarily to derive from this general feature of Johnson's style rather than from Shakespeare's writing. The comic and the tragic are not antithetical in Shakespeare; consider, for instance, the case of Lear and the Fool or Macbeth and the porter. Considering this one can appreciate the extent to which certain preoccupations which find expression in Johnson's style prevent any adequate consideration of Shakespeare. Johnson's mind works away from the complications of actuality towards the clear-cut distinctions it is only possible to make in the world of ideas. Hence the predilection for antithetical forms of expression. What is involved is a failure of response arising from a tendency to abstract the mind.

It is this withdrawal from the complexities of life and the consequent failure to acknowledge the values of it—the values instinct in the actual, the particular, the concrete—that suggests a distortion of the sensibility. It is symptomatic of this that Johnson should observe that

> love is only one of many passions, and as it has no great influence upon the sum of life, it has little operation in the dramas of a poet, who caught his ideas from the living world, and exhibited only what he saw before him.[14]

This is such a surprisingly unperceptive remark to make of Shakespeare that one is forced to account for it in terms of the peculiarities of Johnson's own feelings. Just as his remark about Shakespeare's characters,

> their jests are commonly gross, and their pleasantry licentious; neither his gentlemen nor his ladies have much delicacy, nor are sufficiently distinguished from his clowns by an appearance of refined manners,[15]

suggests that we need to scrutinise eighteenth-century 'refinements' and practices of gentility, the criterion of which was that they "sufficiently distinguished" the polite from the vulgar. Such passages conjure up a world in which love is of little moment (in which, presumably, love and marriage are subservient to political—and economic—considerations) and in which there are sharp divisions between the refined and the vulgar. And ultimately it is this social cleavage, between refined and vulgar and between proper relations (e.g. the arranged marriage) and spontaneous affection, which accounts for the sharp antitheses which command Johnson's thinking and find their inevitable expression in his style.

To some extent what has been said of Johnson so far has itself been over-simple, it suggests a degree of consistency which Johnson never achieved. Consider his contention that "the English nation, in the time of Shakespeare, was yet struggling to emerge from barbarity" and his belief that the virtues of Shakespeare are somehow timeless and abstract; then compare this way of thinking with that revealed in his assertion that Shakespeare is a poet "who caught his ideas from the living world, and exhibited only what he saw before him". Whatever construction may be given to this contention it plainly indicates some awareness of the fact that Shakespeare's work has a definite relationship to the world in which he lived and the time in which he wrote. No matter how timeless Shakespeare's achievements are believed to be, the historicity of his work is a fact. What Johnson fails to perceive, because of his strong idealistic bent, is that the permanent value of Shakespeare cannot be dissociated from the permanent value of the way of life which he epitomises. But given the common opinion of Johnson's time (and of Johnson himself), that the age of Shakespeare was one of semi-barbarity, Johnson does his best to extricate Shakespeare from the general censure. In this he is hamstrung at the outset by common opinion, by that very commitment which gives his utterances their weight and authority. At the same time his tendency to abstract, in this case to abstract the virtues of Shakespeare from the world of Shakespeare, prevents him from realising that the very achievement of Shakespeare is what a lawyer would call 'best' evidence against the barbarity of his age.

We find other signs of this pull of the specific against the stream of abstraction in the *Preface*. Johnson's claim that "Shakespeare approximates the remote, and familiarizes the wonderful"[16] is a most pertinent example. This particularisation which is remarked in Shakespeare, this concern for the specific and familiar, is an essential quality of his greatness. And yet it is one which points away from Johnson's explanation of Shakespeare's durability; a durability attained by sloughing off the particular in Shakespeare and retaining a sense of the abstract propriety of his work, as when Johnson observes that "justice is a virtue independent on time or place".

It would be an injustice to Johnson to overlook the real evidence occasionally displayed of a mind that feels the undercurrents of real, particularised, experience; just as it would be unjust to believe that the common opinion which in so many ways he expresses is merely wrong-headed and misinformed. That it misinformed Johnson in a multitude of particulars is obvious, as when, in the face of Elizabethan literature, a literature of great variety implying a readership at all social levels, he can remark that

> The publick was gross and dark; and to be able to read and write, was an accomplishment still valued for its rarity.[17]

Or when, impervious to the fact that Elizabethan drama is invariably poetic (as that of the eighteenth century is not) he can assert that

> Those to whom our authour's labours were exhibited had more skill in pomps or processions than in poetical language . . .[18]

But allowing all this, allowing also the main current of idealism, the desire for precept and the suspicion of spontaneous life, there is yet a quality of eighteenth-century common sense in Johnson's prose that commends it to our serious attention and places it in firm opposition to the cynicism of Swift.

However much one may disagree with Johnson this disagreement does not cloud the fact of his awareness that what he was writing about was important. This is what the moral tone of his criticism and cast of his writing testifies to: a sense of the general significance of literature, an awareness that the value of literature cannot finally be distinguished from that of all the other pursuits which instruct us towards the achievement of a worthwhile existence. We may believe, and have good grounds for believing, that Johnson has an inadequate perception of the values that inform a good life, but he did perceive that literature and the values of literature were not side issues, that the function of literature and the function of criticism are essentially instructive; as he puts it, "the end of writing is to instruct; the end of poetry is to instruct by pleasing".[19]

This is to make literature a matter of some importance, to see at the centre of all literature the question "How should we live?" It is the sense of this question, never consciously formulated in the *Preface*, that leads Johnson to refer continually outside the immediate frame of Shakespeare's work to the character of Elizabethan England, to what he takes to be its barbarity, its grossness and ignorance. Shakespeare for Johnson is limited by an inadequate perception of the good life. I think this may well be the direction in which his remark that Shakespeare "seems to write without any moral purpose" points.

For Johnson Shakespeare too often accepts the limited conditions of his time; this is borne out by his remark about the lack of delicacy in many of Shakespeare's ladies and gentlemen (Johnson's own limitations are implicit in the sense that needs to be given to 'ladies' and 'gentlemen').*

There can be little doubt as to the seriousness of this kind of criticism of Shakespeare since any attempt to reply to it requires us to re-appraise "the good life". In countering the criticism of the grossness of speech of Shakespeare's ladies and gentlemen one has to counter the presumption that a proper organisation of social life is one in which, in the lines of Clare,

> Proud distinction makes a wider space
> Between the genteel and the vulgar race.

And the pertinence of such a counter-criticism would rely upon such an insight as that which led R. H. Tawney to remark that

> The difference between the England of Shakespeare, still visited by the ghosts of the Middle Ages, and the England which emerged in 1700 from the fierce polemics of the last two generations, was a difference of social and political theory even more than of constitutional arrangements. Not only the facts, but the minds which appraised them, were profoundly modified. The essence of the change was the disappearance of the idea that social institutions and economic activities were related to common ends, which gave them their significance and which served as their criterion.[20]

One has, in arguing against Johnson at any serious level, to favour a different kind of social life from that which he commends; one has to favour a social life informed by a common culture, a common language, in all by a common attitude, and with a degree of mutuality amongst its members such as Johnson finds repugnant in Shakespeare. But it is precisely because it directly involves all this, because it places literature in the centre of life, that Johnson's criticism is of importance. It is this placing of literature which makes the weightiness of tone something more than pompousness and the complacency of utterance something more than mere self-satisfaction; the satisfaction reflects an assurance of rightness in such a placing of literature.

* According to Dryden in his *Essay on Dramatic Poesy* the Elizabethans could produce nothing "which expresses so much the conversation of gentleman, as Sir John Suckling".

2. THE HISTORY OF RASSELAS, PRINCE OF ABYSSINIA

Rasselas is a more explicit statement of the problem encountered in the presumptions of the *Preface to Shakespeare*: How should we live? But because it is more explicit it reveals more clearly the limitations of the *Preface*. When Imlac, the poet, is discoursing upon "the business of the poet" in Chapter 10 we encounter a clearer statement of the measure applied to Shakespeare in the *Preface*.

> The business of a poet, said Imlac, is to examine, not the individual, but the species; to remark general properties and large appearances: he does not number the streaks of the tulip, or describe the different shades in the verdure of the forest. He is to exhibit in his portraits of nature such prominent and striking features, as recall the original to every mind; and must neglect the minuter discriminations, which one may have remarked, and another neglected, for those character-isticks, which are alike obvious to vigilance and carelessness.

"He must," continues Imlac,

> divest himself of the prejudices of his age or country; he must con-sider right and wrong in their abstracted and invariable state; he must disregard present laws and opinions, and rise to general and transcendental truths, which will always be the same.[1]

Here, plainly, is a statement bearing directly upon that tendency to abstract the mind which has been noted in the *Preface*. It is more than this, however. It is a statement such as one might take to heart in appraising the actual performance of eighteenth-century poets, the actual character of their poetry. As a critical and poetical position its weaknesses are apparent. The need to express truths so immediately acceptable to all and sundry leads to the cultivation of the commonplace and the platitudinous; and, indeed, much that we find in *Rasselas* is of that order. Furthermore, the implementation of such dictates as these, with their emphasis upon the need to "neglect the minuter dis-criminations", leads naturally to a failure of discrimination and so to a general coarsening of the attention in which "vigilance and careless-ness" are confused, the one recommending itself as highly as the other. It is with this point of view in mind that we need to appreciate Words-worth's insistence upon the particular, upon truth and insight being concrete and specific rather than abstract and general.

The poetic doctrine of Imlac, however, is drawn from a more fundamental doctrine, as has already been seen in the *Preface*. It is based upon the belief that Reason, which at the time was thought of as a faculty, is essentially a means of abstracting from reality certain observations and refining these into general truths. Reason was thought to be essentially contemplative in its relations with the world about it. Therefore, the poet, in behaving as Imlac prescribes, is a rational creature, subjugating the imagination, the fancy and the passions in order to transmit truths uncoloured by time and place and contemplating the world with detachment. This is the opinion which so impresses Rasselas in Chapter 18. He is present at a public lecture in which a "wise and happy man"

> shewed, with great strength of sentiment, and variety of illustration, that human nature is degraded and debased, when the lower faculties predominate over the higher; that when fancy, the parent of passion, usurps the dominion of the mind, nothing ensures but the natural effect of unlawful government, perturbation and confusion; that she betrays the fortresses of the intellect to rebels, and excites her children to sedition against reason their lawful sovereign. He compared reason to the sun, of which the light is constant, uniform, and lasting; and fancy to a meteor, of bright but transitory lustre, irregular in its motion, and delusive in its direction.

A little later

> He enumerated many examples of heroes immoveable by pain or pleasure, who looked with indifference on those modes or accidents to which the vulgar give the names of good and evil.[2]

Reason, it will be observed, is supreme and feelings likely to interfere in its operations must be vigorously put down. A rational being reflects upon the turbulence of life and the particular occasions of joy and sorrow exist for him simply as objects of contemplation.

Much impressed by the lecture, Rasselas contrives to visit the wise and happy man only to find him distracted by grief at the death of his daughter. The pressures of life which, it seemed, could be distanced in reasoned argument have provided their own bitter refutation of the wise man's teachings. Rasselas is greatly put out.

> "Sir, said the prince, mortality is an event by which a wise man can never be surprised; we know that death is always near, and it should therefore always be expected." "Young man, answered the philosopher, you speak like one that has never felt the pangs of separation." "Have you then forgot the precepts, said Rasselas, which you so powerfully enforced? Has wisdom no strength to arm the heart

against calamity? Consider, that external things are naturally variable, but truth and reason are always the same." "What comfort, said the mourner, can truth and reason afford me? Of what effect are they now, but to tell me, that my daughter will not be restored?"[3]

Rasselas is extraordinarily naïve throughout, but here that naïvety comes out as a lack of sympathy. It is true that we are told he does not, out of humanity, press the point any further, but leaves the wise man and carries with him a conviction of the "emptiness of rhetorical sound",[4] yet even this response reveals the absence of sympathetic feeling. What is touched upon here is that peculiar distortion of sensibility met with in the *Preface*. The instance of the wise man is not an ironic comment by Johnson upon the inadequacy of the doctrine of Reason but an illustration of rationalism betrayed by the weakness of one of its exponents.

That the situation is as it has been described—not a rejection of rationalism but a rejection of the frailty of the wise man—is evident in the response of Rasselas. But lest we have any doubts about this, we find Imlac reiterating the wise man's doctrine much later, in Chapter 44, when he is remarking upon the astronomer who believes he has been entrusted with the direction of the weather.

> Disorders of intellect, answered Imlac, happen much more often than superficial observers will easily believe. Perhaps, if we speak with rigorous exactness, no human mind is in its right state. There is no man whose imagination does not sometimes predominate over his reason, who can regulate his attention wholly by his will, and whose ideas will come and go at his command. No man will be found in whose mind airy notions do not sometimes tyrannise, and force him to hope or fear beyond the limits of sober probability. All power of fancy over reason is a degree of insanity; but while this power is such as we can controul and repress, it is not visible to others, nor considered as any depravation of the mental faculties: it is not pronounced madness but when it becomes ungovernable, and apparently influences speech or action.[5]

Reason, then, is still supreme, a faculty to which all other faculties should be subject even though in actual fact they seldom are. The ideal is still that whose consequences are seen in Rasselas' reaction to the grief of the wise man. One can point to the inadequacy of this simply by remarking that grief is not an intrusion upon sanity but a necessary expression of it: "Solon, when he wept for his son's death, and one said to him, 'Weeping will not help,' answered, 'Alas, therefore I weep, because weeping will not help.' "[6]

The character of the history itself provides a further indication of Johnson's own subscription to the doctrine of Reason. Rasselas, his sister and Imlac attempt to distinguish between the merits of different modes of life by observation; they are not participants but tourists in the world. The mode of procedure is well expressed in the chapter in which they set out to visit the pyramids (Ch. 31).

> They travelled gently, turned aside to every thing remarkable, stopped from time to time and conversed with the inhabitants, and observed the various appearances of towns, ruined and inhabited, of wild and cultivated nature.[7]

And so the party meander along, contemplating the world about them and generalising upon it in passing judgment. This mode of procedure, in what is intended as an investigation into the conditions of human happiness, is an allegory of rational conduct. The allegory, however, takes us beyond the doctrine of Reason to some consideration of its basis and in particular its basis in social life.

Rasselas, Imlac and the princess are fortunate instruments for the exposition of such a doctrine. Although the life of observation and contemplation which they lead may be thought ideal, it is based upon a very important condition and it is because they are able to fulfil this condition, or rather can be made to do so by Johnson, that they satisfy the needs of exposition. The condition is met very simply, in Chapter 15:

> This prince and princess had jewels sufficient to make them rich whenever they came into a place of commerce, which, by Imlac's direction, they hid in their cloaths.[8]

From the moment they enter the world the travellers are free from the cares of material well-being and so fulfil the basic requirement of the allegory. Simultaneously, however, they serve to indicate that the doctrine they allegorise is one which commends itself to leisure rather than to business. That this is so is everywhere apparent in *Rasselas*, but it is particularly noticeable in the displacement of happiness from the normal pursuits of life.

The pursuit of felicity is presented as an essential ingredient in the choice of life—the notion that people have such a choice is a clue to Johnson's social horizons—and yet felicity proves most elusive, so elusive that the history ends with "The Conclusion, in which nothing is concluded". It is surely not surprising to anyone, except Rasselas and Co., that if happiness is abstracted into leisure it becomes a phantom without any real substance. The failure to locate happiness lies in this constriction of the intelligence imposed by rationalism rather than in the non-existence of happiness amongst men. Happiness, one is prompted to declare, is not a state that can be divorced from the multifarious activities, with their concomitant feelings and dispositions, which make up the stuff of life. The search for a happy life ignores this, although it is a fact attested to even by the observations of Rasselas and his companions. That they ignore it is due to a presumption which places Happiness, Sorrow, Knowledge, and similar abstractions, as more real, because in some sense more durable, than the actual conditions of life out of which they arise. Happiness itself, as other dispositions of the feelings, is not, from what one observes even in *Rasselas*, an aim of life, not a tangible result of leading this or that kind of life, but a subsidiary to the business of living.

This clearly bears upon the distortion of sensibility we meet with in Johnson. In the case of happiness it is a result of confusing a feeling with a mental abstraction. But this confusion is itself the result of a condition of life divorced from the problems and pressures of material well-being and given over to their contemplation. In such an existence, happiness becomes a pursuit of leisure rather than a consequence of life-creating activity. It is seen as something that can be hunted for as an end-in-itself. It ceases to be appreciated as a quality of existence and comes to be seen as a state of mind.

I think one now begins to see more clearly the relationship between Johnsonian attitudes of mind, such as these are revealed in the *Preface* and more explicitly in *Rasselas*, and the social conditions prevailing at the time. What plainly dominates Johnson's thinking and responses are the dominant opinions and dispositions of his age, those of polite society, that is to say of a class removed from the common businesses of life and, for the same reasons as Rasselas and Co., capable of leading a leisured existence and of reflecting upon life in comfort. This can be more particularly substantiated by considering the kind of opinions that are encountered and the kind of attitudes that are met with in *Rasselas*.

Love, it is remarked in the *Preface to Shakespeare*, is not a particularly important part of life. It wasn't important, I suggested earlier, because for Johnson there was a distinction between the politico-economic relationship of man to woman and the affectional one and because for him and his contemporaries it was the former which was important in determining the relation of the sexes. As Johnson enables us to see, this emphasis is by no means irrational:

> What [asks Rasselas in Ch. 29] can be expected but disappointment and repentance from a choice made in the immaturity of youth, in the ardour of desire, without judgement, without foresight, without enquiry after conformity of opinions, similarity of manners, rectitude of judgment, or purity of sentiment? Such is the common process of marriage. A youth and maiden meeting by chance, or brought together by artifice, exchange glances, reciprocate civilities, go home, and dream of one another. Having little to divert attention, or diversify thought, they find themselves uneasy when they are apart, and therefore conclude that they shall be happy together.[9]

Although the recurrent presumption of leisure is present—the people concerned have "little to divert attention or diversify thought"—this passage expresses quite well the rational view of what too frequently passed for the love relationship. Not until our own century in fact has romantic love been generally considered a proper basis for marriage; in the great age of romance, from the twelfth to the sixteenth centuries, its end was adultery rather than marital union. The criticism of the rational view is that it considers marriage as a contrived relationship; the most intimate of all human connections is thus laid upon a basis of computation.

But I suppose it is now evident what kind of general objection I am levelling against the attitude of mind expressed in *Rasselas*, an attitude particularly noticeable in this instance because it does bear upon the most intimate of human relationships. My objection is that Johnson drives a wedge between the cultivation of the reason and the cultivation of the feelings and, more pertinently, that he often confuses matters of reason with matters of feeling. He is led to this by placing reason and the rule of reason above the passions and by seeing the passions not as an essential human dynamic that needs to be carefully cultivated but as a power of subversion threatening reason. The result is a perversion of natural feeling. When David Hume protests that reason is and ought only to be the slave of the passions he is similarly guilty of boxing-up the personality. Both Johnson and Hume fall victims of the same desire to abstract and so reduce the complexities of life to a manageable formula. At times the result can be comic, as when Rasselas asserts in all his naïve seriousness,

Whenever I shall seek a wife, it shall be my first question, whether she be willing to be led by reason?[10]

Whereas, one feels, the first question should be whether she will be a good wife. That someone is rational is no guarantee that he will put that rationality to good ends, he might as readily use it to accomplish evil ones.

But it would be unfair to Johnson not to observe that he anticipates the objections to Rasselas's decision in the princess's retort to her brother's declaration.

Thus it is, said Nekayah, that philosophers are deceived. There are a thousand familiar disputes which reason never can decide; questions that elude investigation, and make logick ridiculous; cases where something must be done, and where little can be said. Consider the state of mankind, and enquire how few can be supposed to act upon any occasions, whether small or great, with all the reasons of action present to their minds. Wretched would be the pair above all names of wretchedness, who should be doomed to adjust by reason every morning all the minute detail of a domestick day.[11]

Difficulties do not pass unnoticed, therefore, although they do not undermine the general standards prescribed by the history.

These general standards are, in ways I have already tried to suggest, largely dependent upon an appeal to a particular kind of life, one which has the gift of leisure and is emancipated from the need to undertake the minute details of a domestic day and, in particular, is free from the necessity of procuring the means of life. In view of this special basis in life, it is not surprising that in the course of the history views are encountered which express this bias, as when Rasselas and his companions encounter the shepherds in Chapter 19. Instead of discovering the shepherds enjoying perfect felicity in the pursuit of pastoral pleasures,

it was evident that their hearts were cankered with discontent; that they considered themselves as condemned to labour for the luxury of the rich, and looked up with stupid malevolence towards those that were placed above them.[12]

How unreasonable of them! However, we have already been informed that they are rude and ignorant; we now learn that they are stupid. So we need not pay any serious attention to their opinions nor let them cast the slightest shadow upon "the luxury of the rich", for if they do cast such a shadow it is merely that of their "stupid male-volence". Be aware of the limitations of the ideals of Reason, or at least take with a measure of seriousness some objections levelled against them, but do not for a moment give serious attention to any criticism of the kind of life upon which those ideals depend! That would be malevolent stupidity! If it is not stupidity, then it is a fantasy bordering upon madness:

> "I will confess, said the prince, an indulgence of fantastick delight more dangerous than yours. I have frequently endeavoured to image the possibility of a perfect government, by which all wrong should be restrained, all vice reformed, and all the subjects preserved in tranquillity and innocence. This thought produced innumerable schemes of reformation, and dictated many useful regulations and salutary edicts . . ."
>
> "Such, says Imlac, are the effects of visionary schemes: when we first form them we know them to be absurd, but familiarise them by degrees, and in time lose sight of their folly."[13]

It seems fitting to conclude this tentative view of literature and the rise of capitalism here, with what could so easily be an imaginary dialogue between More and Johnson on the possibility of a palace revolution.

It is, however, an imaginary dialogue written out of the complacency of the eighteenth-century establishment. What it lacks is any real sense of civilised life, any awareness of the communality of human interest we find in More, Shakespeare, and Jonson, and it is this which makes it such a fitting expression of the new order of things.

Reference Notes

1. MORE'S *UTOPIA*

1. The text of Wyatt's poems is taken from *Collected Poems of Sir Thomas Wyatt*, ed. Kenneth Muir and Patricia Thomson (Liverpool, 1969).
2. Thomas More, *Utopia and a Dialogue of Comfort*, intr. John Warrington (Everyman Library, 1951), pp. 81–2.
3. More, p. 80.
4. More, pp. 23, 27, 28.
5. More, p. 66.
6. More, p. 133.
7. More, pp. 132–3.
8. More, p. 133.
9. More, pp. 26–7.
10. More, p. 29.
11. More, pp. 42–3.
12. More, p. 94.
13. More, p. 82.

2. LOVE POETRY IN THE SIXTEENTH CENTURY
1. The Coming of the Golden Age

1. Raymond Southall, *The Courtly Maker* (Oxford, 1964), pp. 148 *et seq.*
2. Southall, p. 159.
3. Thomas Starkey, *A Dialogue Between Reginald Pole and Thomas Lupset*, ed. Kathleen M. Burton (London, 1948), p. 81.
4. More, p. 133. D. H. Lawrence, "Study of Thomas Hardy" in *Phoenix*, ed. Edward D. McDonald (London, 1936), p. 428.
5. James M. Osborn, ed., *The Autobiography of Thomas Whythorne* (Oxford, 1961), p. 140.
6. Whythorne, p. 140.
7. Thorstein Veblen, *The Theory of the Leisure Class* (New York, 1953), p. 229.
8. Karl Marx, *Economic and Philosophic Manuscripts of 1844* (London, 1959), p. 101.
9. D. H. Lawrence, "Morality and the Novel" in *Phoenix*, p. 531.
10. Samuel Johnson, "Preface to Shakespeare" in *Shakespeare Criticism: A Selection*, intr. D. Nicholl Smith (London, 1916), p. 94.
11. Plato, *The Symposium*, tr. W. Hamilton (London, 1951), p. 40.
12. *The Poems of Sir Philip Sidney*, ed. William A. Ringler, Jr. (Oxford, 1962), p. 105.
13. R. H. Tawney, *Religion and the Rise of Capitalism* (London, 1938), p. 130.
14. *Elizabethan Lyrics*, ed. Norman Ault (London, 1925). Lyrics quoted are from this collection unless otherwise stated.
15. Veblen, p. 96.
16. See Thomas Morley's "See, see, mine own sweet jewel" in *Canzonets* (1593); Shakespeare's *Romeo and Juliet*, I.v.50; Skoloker's "Her Praises" in *Diaphantus* (1604); and,

later, Sylvester's sonnet "They say that shadows of deceased ghosts", *Posthumi* in *Du Bartas* (1633).

17. Veblen, p. 95.
18. *Astrophil and Stella*, sonnet 37.
19. *Astrophil and Stella*, sonnet 36.
20. *Astrophil and Stella*, sonnet 16.
21. Rosemund Tuve, *Elizabethan and Metaphysical Imagery* (Chicago, 1947), p. 3.
22. J. R. Hale, *England and the Italian Renaissance* (London, 1963), p. 29.
23. Whythorne, pp. 139–40.
24. William Rankins, *Seven Satires* (1598), "Satyr quintus", line 25.
25. Drummond, "Alexis, here she stayed"; Rankins, *op. cit.*, "Satyrus peregrinans", lines 45–6; Lyly, "Daphne"; Lodge, "Rosalind"; Greene, "Samela"; Warner, "My Mistress"; Marston, "Delicious Beauty that doth lie"; Drummond, "The ivory, coral, gold".
26. Spenser, "Fayre is my loue, when her fayre golden heares" and *Epithalamion*, lines 154–6, in *The Poetical Works of Edmund Spenser*, ed. J. C. Smith and E. De Selincourt (Oxford, 1924).
27. Sidney, *Astrophil and Stella*, Sonnet 23; Dyer, "Coridon to his Phyllis' in *England's Helicon* (1600); F. Pilkington, "Have I found her?" in *Madrigals and Pastorals* (1613).

2. Putting on the Style

1. Wyatt, CLXV.
2. Tuve, p. 6.
3. George Puttenham, *The Arte of English Poesie*, ed. G. D. Willcock and Alice Walker (Cambridge, 1936), pp. 137–8.
4. Thomas Wilson, *The Arte of Rhetorick*, ed. G. H. Mair (Oxford, 1909), p. 162.
5. Spenser, "June Aeglogue", lines 81–2.
6. Victor Harris and Itrat Husain, *English Prose, 1600–1660* (New York, 1965), p. 346.
7. Petrarch, *Selected Poems*, ed. T. Gwynfor Griffiths and P. R. J. Hainsworth (Manchester U.P., 1971), p. 43.
8. *King Lear*, III.iv.108–12.
9. Veblen, p. 121.
10. William Harrison, *Description of England* (1587) quoted in John Dover Wilson, *Life in Shakespeare's England* (1944), p. 165.
11. Jonson, Harris and Husain, pp. 332–3.
12. Jonathan Swift, *A Tale of A Tub and Other Satires* (Everyman Library, London 1963), p. 56.
13. Jonson, Harris and Husain, p. 348.
14. Jonson, Harris and Husain, p. 335.
15. Samuel Daniel, *The Complaint of Rosamond* (1592), lines 549 and 528; Shakespeare, Sonnet 54; J. C., "The Frailty of Beauty", in Ault, p. 216.
16. Barnes, "The world's bright comforter, whose beamsome"; Rogers, "The Spirit of Night", in Ault, pp. 215, 245.
17. Davies, *Hymns to Astraea* (1599), Hymn VII.
18. Davies, *op. cit.*, Hymn III; Drummond, "What doth it serve to see sun's burning face", in Ault, pp. 270–1, 467.
19. Anon., "Clear or cloudy, sweet as April showering"; Fitzgeffry, "The Bee", in Ault, pp. 302, 228.
20. *Canzoniere*, CXCII, line 5.
21. Sidney, "An Apology for Poetry", in *English Critical Essays*, ed. Edmund D. Jones (Oxford, 1952), p. 7.

22. Tawney, p 111.
23. Karl Marx, *Economic and Philosophic Manuscripts of 1844* (London, 1959), p. 119.
24. Whythorne, p. 23. See also the third part of the "Homily against Peril of Idolatory", in *Certain Sermons or Homilies Appointed to be read in Churches in the time of Queen Elizabeth* (London, 1846), p. 272.
25. Puttenham, p. 299.
26. Whythorne, p. 65.
27. Quoted by William Haller, *The Rise of Puritanism* (New York, 1957), p. 140.
28. Whythorne, p. 23; Thomas Nashe, "Pierce Penilesse His Supplication to the Devil", in *Three Elizabethan Pamphlets*, ed. G. R. Hibbard (London, 1951), p. 157.
29. Quoted from the Churchwardens' accounts by Henry Gee, *The Elizabethan Prayer-Book and Ornaments* (1902), p. 147.

3. The Commerce of Affection

1. *Idea*, Sonnet 28.
2. "Unquiet thoughts, your civil slaughter stint", *First Book of Songs and Airs* (1597).
3. *Seven Satires* (1598), satyr tertius, line 18.
4. Rankins, satyr quintus, line 38.
5. Davies of Hereford, "It is as true as strange, else trial feigns".
6. Sidney, "My true love hath my hart".
7. Chapman, "Epithalamion Terates"; Anon., "Silly Boy, there is no cause".
8. From John Wilbye's *Madrigals* (1598) in *Lyrics from Elizabethan Song Books*, ed. A. H. Bullen (London, 1891).
9. Shakespeare, *Troilus and Cressida*, II.i.51–2.
10. Rankins, satyr septimus, lines 16–18, and note.
11. Rankins, satyrus peregrinians, lines 71–5.
12. Robert Burton, *The Anatomy of Melancholy*, (London, 1927), p. 529.
13. Jonson, *Volpone*, I.i.
14. C. L. Barber, *Shakespeare's Festive Comedy* (Princeton, 1959), pp. 166–7.
15. Richard Barnfield, "The Encomion of Lady Pecunia: or the Praise of Money", in *Some Longer Elizabethan Poems*, intr. A. H. Bullen (London, 1903). Lady Pecunia is also a character in Ben Jonson's *The Staple News*.

4. The New Religion

1. "Prologue to the Canterbury Tales", lines 443–4, in *The Works of Geoffrey Chaucer*, ed. F. N. Robinson (London, 1957).
2. See Pliny, *Historia Naturalis*, XXXIII, 19.
3. "Elegy XVIII, Love's Progress".
4. John Wheeler, *A Treatise of Commerce* (1601), Facsimile Text Society (New York, 1931), p. 6.
5. Helen C. White, *Social Criticism in Popular Religious Literature of the Sixteenth Century* (New York, 1965), p. 193.
6. "Of the True Greatness of the Kingdom of Britain", in *Works*, ed. Spedding, Ellis and Heath, III, 55.
7. Richard Barnfield, *The Shepheards Content* (1594).
8. *Certain Sermons or Homilies*, p. 53.
9. William Haller, *The Rise of Puritanism* (New York, 1957), p. 117.
10. *Certain Sermons or Homilies*, p. 82.
11. F.B.P., "Jerusalem, my happy home", *The Song of Mary* (1601).
12. Raleigh, "The Passionate Man's Pilgrimage", *Diaphantus* (1604).
13. Donne, "Elegy XIX, To His Mistress Going to Bed", and Shakespeare, Sonnet 52.

14. Rankins, "Spes Imperfecta".
15. Barnfield, see §, n. 15, above. Burton, pp. 33–4.
16. Wheeler, p. 7.
17. Thomas Dekker, *The Seven Deadly Sinnes of London*, 1606 (London, 1905), p. 63.
18. *The Wandering Jew telling Fortunes to Englishmen* (1649), quoted by Louis B. Wright, p. 199.
19. *Timon of Athens*, IV.iii.26–34.
20. Karl Marx, *Economic and Philosophic Manuscripts of 1844* (London, 1959), p. 139.
21. *Volpone*, I.i.14–18.
22. Thomas Dekker, "The Wonderful Year", in *Three Elizabethan Pamphlets*, p. 176.
23. G. L. Brook (ed.) *The Harley Lyrics* (Manchester, 1956), p. 9.
24. Dekker, *Seven Deadly Sinnes*, p. 63; Donne, *Sermon Preached at the Funerals of Sir William Cockayne Knight*; Thomas Taylor, *vid.* Haller, p. 159; Wheeler, p. 7.
25. John Russell Brown, *Shakespeare and His Comedies* (London, 1957), pp. 45–6.
26. *Timon of Athens*, IV.iii.35–7, 39–41.
27. *The Staple of News*, II.i.191.
28. "My love, I cannot thy rare beauties place".
29. "Amaryllis".
30. "Adieu! farewell earth's bliss!"
31. *Certain Sonnets*, sonnet 32.
32. Sonnet 146.
33. Sir John Davies, *Orchestra, A Poem of Dancing* (1594), st. 126, and *Hymns of Astraea* (1599), Hymn I.

5. The Shakespearian Diagnosis

1. Anon., "Do not, oh, do not prize", in R. Jones, *Ultimum Vale* (1608)
2. David Lloyd Stevenson, *The Love Game Comedy* (New York, 1946), pp. 11, 12. For the popularity of Ovid in English translation see the editions listed in V. de Sola Pinto, *The English Renaissance* (London, 1951), pp. 185–6.
3. Whythorne, p. 66.
4. J. C. Maxwell, "Shakespeare: The Middle Plays", in *The Age of Shakespeare*, ed. Boris Ford (London, 1955), p. 218.
5. Erich Fromm, *The Fear of Freedom* (London, 1942), pp. 8, 9.
6. Tawney, p. 33.
7. See p. 67 above.
8. Tawney, p. 47.
9. E. M. W. Tillyard, *Shakespeare's Problem Plays* (London, 1951), p. 63.
10. Caroline Spurgeon, *Shakespeare's Imagery* (Cambridge, 1968), p. 316.
11. Starkey, p. 81.
12. *Volpone*, I.i.
13. "The Marxist Perspective", *TLS*, 23 April 1964, p. 348.
14. D. H. Lawrence, "The Overtone", in *The Lovely Lady* (New York, 1946), p. 154.

3. THE ART OF BEING HUMAN

1. The Little World of John Donne

1. Marx, *op. cit.*, p. 104.
2. Psalm 6, *Domine ne infurore*, lines 107–8.

3. "I am a little world made cunningly", in John Donne, *The Divine Poems*, ed. Helen Gardner (Oxford, 1959).
4. John Donne, *The Elegies and The Songs and Sonnets*, ed. Helen Gardner (Oxford, 1965).
5. John Donne, *Devotions Upon Emergent Occasions*, ed. John Sparrow (Cambridge, 1923), "Meditation 10".
6. Victor Harris and Itrat Husain, *English Prose, 1600–1660* (New York, 1965), p. 280.
7. John Donne, *Selected Prose*, chosen by Evelyn Simpson, ed. Helen Gardner and Timothy Healy (Oxford, 1967), p. 281.
8. *Elegies and Songs and Sonnets.*
9. *Elegies and Songs and Sonnets.*
10. *Divine Poems.*
11. Harris and Husain, p. 254.
12. Harris and Husain, p. 254.
13. Harris and Husain, p. 255.
14. *Elegies and Songs and Sonnets.*
15. "An Elegie upon the death of the Deane of Pauls, Dr. John Donne", lines 95–6, in *The Poems of Thomas Carew*, ed. Rhodes Dunlop (Oxford, 1964).
16. *Elegies and Songs and Sonnets.*
17. T. S. Eliot, *Selected Essays* (London, 1951), pp. 288–9.
18. *Selected Prose*, p. 281.
19. *Devotions*, p. 52.
20. John A. T. Robinson, *Honest to God* (London, 1963), pp. 48–9.
21. *Elegies and Songs and Sonnets.*
22. *Divine Poems.*
23. *Devotions*, p. 98.

2. Ben Jonson

1. J. B. Bamborough, *Ben Jonson* (London, 1970), p. 60.
2. All quotations from Jonson are from *Ben Jonson*, ed. C. H. Herford, P. and E. Simpson (Oxford, 1925–52).
3. Prologue to *Cynthia's Revels*.
4. Induction to *Every Man out of his Humour*, lines 119–20.
5. *On my First Sonne*.
6. *To the immortall memorie, and friendship of the noble paire, Sir Lucius Cary and Sir H. Morison*, lines 48–50.
7. *To the memory of my beloved, the Author Mr. William Shakespeare*, line 68.
8. *Timber, or Discoveries, ed. cit.*, VIII, 583.
9. Wordsworth, *Preface to Lyrical Ballads*, William Wordsworth and Samuel Taylor Coleridge, *Lyrical Ballads 1805*, ed. Derek Roper (London, 1968), p. 22.
10. *Essay on Criticism*, II, 362.
11. Bamborough, p. 40.
12. Induction to *Every Man out of his Humour*, lines 121–2.
13. Mammon is a character in *The Alchemist* and Lady Pecunia in *The Staple of News*.
14. One of the finest essays on Jonson's poetry is "The Tone of Ben Jonson's Poetry" in Geoffrey Walton's *Metaphysical to Augustan* (London, 1955).
15. *Poetaster*, III.iv.
16. Bamborough, p. 65.
17. "The Hock-Cart, or Harvest home", *The Poetical Works of Robert Herrick*, ed. L. C. Martin (Oxford, 1963), p. 101.
18. *Op. cit.*, p. 68.

3. Thomas Hobbes

1. Thomas Hobbes, *Leviathan* (Everyman Edn., London 1914), p. 1.
2. *Leviathan*, p. 33.
3. *Leviathan*, p. 34.
4. Starkey, pp. 57–8.
5. *Devotions Upon Emergent Occasions*, p. 98.
6. *Leviathan*, pp. 64–5.
7. *Leviathan*, p. 367.

4. CRISIS AND RESOLUTION

1. Paradise Lost

1. Lord Macaulay, *Critical and Historical Essays*, ed. F. C. Montague (London, 1903), I, 287.
2. *Paradise Lost*, I, 81–94. All references to Milton's poems are to *The Poetical Works of John Milton*, ed. Helen Darbishire, 2 vols. (Oxford, 1952, 1955).
3. *Paradise Lost*, I, 24–6.
4. *Paradise Lost*, VII, 30–1.
5. *Paradise Lost*, VI, 147–8.
6. *Paradise Lost*, VI, 29–37.
7. *Lycidas*, 1–9.
8. *Lycidas*, 37–49.
9. *Lycidas*, 64–84.
10. *Lycidas*, 113–29.
11. *Paradise Lost*, VIII, 15–38.
12. *Paradise Lost*, VIII, 160–1, 167–8.
13. *Paradise Lost*, IX, 103–9.
14. *Paradise Lost*, VIII, 179–87.
15. Richard Baxter, *The Dying Thoughts* (Kelly's edn., London, 1843), p. 582.
16. Baxter, p. 582.
17. Macaulay, I, 27.
18. *Paradise Lost*, VIII, 538–9.
19. *Paradise Lost*, VIII, 546–52.
20. *Paradise Lost*, VIII, 567–70.
21. *Paradise Lost*, VIII, 635–6.
22. *Paradise Lost*, VIII, 494–9.
23. *Paradise Lost*, IX, 913–16, 953–9.
24. *Paradise Lost*, IX, 997–9.
25. *Paradise Lost*, IX, 1182–6.
26. *Paradise Lost*, X, 137–43.
27. *Paradise Lost*, IX, 896–916.
28. *Paradise Lost*, IX, 952–9.
29. *Paradise Lost*, IX, 961.
30. *Paradise Lost*, IX, 1121–9.
31. *Paradise Lost*, IX, 444–51.
32. *Paradise Lost*, IX, 452–66.
33. *Paradise Lost*, 478–9.

2. Pilgrim's Progress

1. *The Works of John Bunyan*, ed. George Offor (Glasgow, Edinburgh, London, 1855), I, lxxvii. All references to Bunyan are to this edition of his works.
2. Offor, III, 99.
3. Offor, I, 57.
4. Offor, III, 129.
5. Offor, III, 130.
6. Offor, III, 131.
7. Offor, III, 17.
8. Offor, III, 109.
9. Offor, III, 111.
10. Offor, III, 119.
11. David W. Petegorsky, *Left-Wing Democracy in the English Civil War*, p. 65.
12. Offor, III, 137.
13. Offor, III, 119–20.
14. Offor, III, 70.
15. *Boswell's Life of Johnson*, II, ed. L. F. Powell (Oxford, 1934), p. 238.
16. Joan Bennett, *Five Metaphysical Poets* (Cambridge, 1964), p. 63.
17. Offor, III, 111.
18. Macaulay, I, 276.
19. Offor, III, 142.
20. Offor, III, 142.
21. Macaulay, I, 286.
22. Macaulay, I, 278.

5. JOHNSON: SHAKESPEARE AND THE PRINCE OF ABYSSINIA

1. Johnson and Shakespeare

1. Karl Jaspers, "The History of Mankind as seen by the Philosopher", *Universitas*, VI, 3 (1964), 220.
2. Macaulay, I, 387, 391.
3. Samuel Johnson, *Rasselas, Poems, and Selected Prose*, ed. Bertrand H. Bronson (New York, 1958), p. 268.
4. Johnson, p. 279.
5. Johnson, p. 239.
6. Johnson, pp. 249–50.
7. L. C. Knights, "How Many Children Had Lady Macbeth?" *Explorations* (London, 1951), p. 18.
8. Johnson, p. 258.
9. Johnson, p. 258.
10. Macaulay, I, 389–90.
11. Johnson, p. 248.
12. Johnson, pp. 247–8.
13. Macaulay, I, 394.
14. Johnson, p. 243.
15. Johnson, p. 250.
16. Johnson, pp. 243–4.
17. Johnson, p. 259.

18. Johnson, p. 260.
19. Johnson, p. 245.
20. R. H. Tawney, *The Acquisitive Society* (London, 1961), p. 17.

2. The History of Rasselas

1. Johnson, pp. 527–8.
2. Johnson, pp. 545–6.
3. Johnson, p. 546.
4. Johnson, p. 547.
5. Johnson, pp. 595–6.
6. Bacon, *Apophthegms*, 194.
7. Johnson, p. 570.
8. Johnson, p. 538.
9. Johnson, p. 565.
10. Johnson, p. 566.
11. Johnson, pp. 566–7.
12. Johnson, p. 547.
13. Johnson, p. 597.

Index

Index